# The ELEARNING DESIGNER'S Handbook

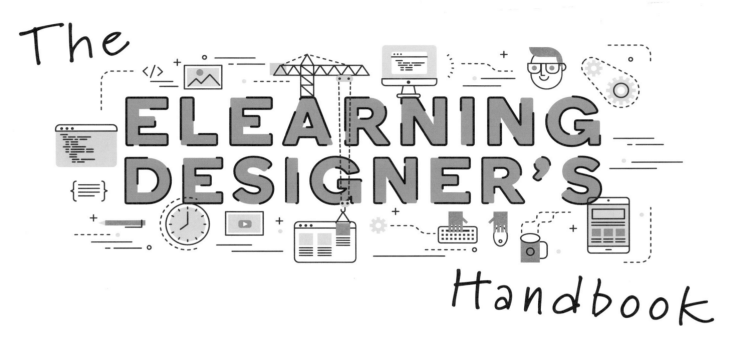

A practical guide to the eLearning development process for eLearning designers.

^ NEW!

# BY TIM SLADE

"The second edition of *The eLearning Designer's Handbook* is a fantastic primer for those new to the field. It addresses instructional design fundamentals, eLearning development tools, and even gets into more advanced topics like needs analysis, prototyping, and evaluation. It walks you through everything you need to consider when building a course. Experienced designers will also appreciate this thoughtful refresher of the best practices we should all be doing every day!"

- Carla Torgerson, Director of Instructional Design at Bull City Learning

"The second edition of *The eLearning Designer's Handbook* is as close to the experience of finding a great work mentor as you can get in book format! In it, Tim shares the essential eLearning design and development processes you'll want to know as you get started (including his insights on how things actually play out in the real world), all the while continually making sure you feel like you've got this! This book won't just help you survive your first eLearning projects: it'll help you feel confident you're taking all the right steps along the way."

- Bianca Woods, Senior Manager of Programming at The Learning Guild

"If you're new to the world of eLearning, there is an overwhelming body of knowledge available. The second edition of *The eLearning Designer's Handbook* offers useful information about instructional theories, principles, and models to support the creation of effective eLearning. With years of experience, Tim compiles the essentials and lays out an organized plan to begin your journey to become a successful eLearning designer and developer."

- Kevin Thorn, CLEO at NuggetHead Studioz

"The second edition of *The eLearning Designer's Handbook* is an absolute instructional and visual delight! If you are just getting started with eLearning, this book is custom-made for you. It will help you get answers to all the possible questions about the eLearning design and development process. Be ready to explore some wonderful opportunities to reflect and pen down your own thoughts, experiences, and plans while talking to Tim about his eLearning journey!"

- Dr. Pooja Jaisingh, Lead eLearning Evangelist at Adobe

The eLearning Designer's Handbook:
A Practical Guide to the eLearning Development Process for New eLearning Designers | Second Edition
by Tim Slade

Tim Slade
www.timslade.com
www.elearningacademy.io
tim@timslade.com

ISBN: 9798615125300

This book is dedicated to all of you who never dreamed of becoming eLearning designers, yet somehow fell into it and learned to love it.

# CONTENTS

# CONTENTS

# NO ONE DREAMS OF BECOMING AN ELEARNING DESIGNER.

**Allow me to explain.**

I've never truly considered myself a real learning professional, let alone an eLearning professional. Although I've spent the last decade working in the field of eLearning, I still feel relatively new to the industry. I think a lot of this has to do with how I fell into eLearning in the first place.

You see, my eLearning career started while I was working in retail a few years out of high school. A new mall had recently opened in my hometown of Prescott, Arizona, and it was a prime location for all the twenty-somethings to find a job.

I was quickly hired at Dillard's, where I started working in the Men's Clothing Department. After several months of working on commission, selling overpriced clothes to rude customers, I was given the opportunity to join the Loss Prevention Team. At the time, I wasn't entirely sure what loss prevention was, but I jumped at the opportunity to get off the sales floor. Rather than trying to catch my sales quota, I was now catching shoplifters.

My job was pretty simple: sit in a tiny office, watch cameras, and catch shoplifters. I always like to say loss prevention is one step up from being a mall cop, but that never bothered me—not only was I good at catching shoplifters, I also enjoyed it tremendously.

**This is how I fell into the world of eLearning.**

I continued working in the field of loss prevention for the next six years, moving between a few different retailers along the way. I eventually ended up at Kohl's Department Stores as a Loss Prevention Supervisor. I didn't realize it at the time, but my career (and life) was about to change dramatically.

While working at Kohl's, I was offered the unique opportunity to join the Kohl's Corporate Loss Prevention Team in Milwaukee, Wisconsin. At the time, I knew this was my opportunity to jump into a salaried position and further my loss prevention career—I was now going to be a "corporate guy" with a career trajectory. I even earned my undergraduate degree in Criminal Justice.

## No one dreams of becoming an eLearning designer.

During that first year in my new job, everything changed. I helped develop an onboarding program for new loss prevention employees and single-handedly created a series of eLearning courses on how to catch shoplifters. I learned how to use my first eLearning authoring tool (Articulate Studio '09) and several graphic design tools. I also uncovered hidden talents for presentation design and visual communications.

After settling into my first eLearning job at Kohl's, I quickly realized I was no longer viewed as the "corporate loss prevention guy." I was now "the guy who could make things look pretty on the screen." Although I was still working within the Loss Prevention Department, loss prevention was no longer my function—just the subject of my work, which was now eLearning and graphic design.

That's me!

*Here I am in 2009 with the actors and film crew in a Kohl's store, shooting shoplifting scenes for my first eLearning project.*

### Does your journey into eLearning sound similar?

After realizing I was no longer a loss prevention professional, but rather an eLearning professional, it took me years to fully appreciate that my journey into eLearning was *not* unique. After attending countless conferences and interacting with hundreds of other eLearning professionals, I realized that most of them faced the same career identity crisis of becoming an eLearning designer as I did.

The truth is, if your journey into eLearning was anything like mine, your career didn't start in eLearning. Although you might be working as an eLearning designer now, you likely had an entirely different career before falling into eLearning.

## Who is this book for?

I decided to write this book because I know what it's like to be in your shoes. I know what it's like to face the challenges of becoming an eLearning designer without having the slightest idea of what that even means.

I wrote this book for folks who want and need a step-by-step guide for building and managing an eLearning project. I wrote this book to help you understand the differences between a storyboard and a prototype, a subject matter expert and a stakeholder, and everything in between.

While I hope this book is helpful in your journey to becoming an eLearning designer, it's certainly not the be-all, end-all of eLearning or instructional design books. As you grow your skills, make sure to expand your knowledge by expanding your resources beyond this one book.

# What Do You Think?

Did you have a career before you fell into eLearning or instructional design? If so, what was it?

_____

_____

_____

When did you realize you wanted to transition your career into eLearning or instructional design?

_____

_____

_____

What struggles did you face (or are currently facing) when you first started?

_____

_____

_____

If you could do it all over again, what would you do differently?

_____

_____

_____

# WHY MOST ELEARNING FAILS *and Sucks!*

---

**In this chapter, you'll explore...**

- Why most eLearning fails.
- The cost of bad eLearning.
- How to design better eLearning.

# NOTES

_____

_____

_____

_____

_____

_____

_____

_____

_____

_____

_____

_____

_____

_____

_____

_____

_____

# WHY MOST ELEARNING FAILS and Sucks!

**My first eLearning project was a total disaster!**

I remember when I was tasked with my very first eLearning project. I had to create a five-part course on the steps for apprehending a shoplifter within a retail environment. While I knew a lot about catching shoplifters, I knew very little about designing and developing an eLearning course. I remember feeling lost, confused, and unsure about where to begin. I recall my boss at the time giving me a list of names and asking me to partner with them on the content. She kept referring to these folks as "SMEs and stakeholders." And to be honest, I really had no idea what a SME or stakeholder was—let alone the difference between the two!

The truth is, my story isn't unique. Most of the folks working in our industry fell into it entirely by accident—they were good at something, and one day someone said they should train others to do that thing. While this phenomenon has created a lot of diversity within our industry (which is a good thing), it has also led to many folks being ill-equipped with the skills and know-how to create engaging, performance-based eLearning.

## Why Does Most eLearning Fail?

Here's my honest opinion: I think most eLearning sucks. I really do! And yes, I know that seems like a pretty bold statement; however, please don't get me wrong. I don't say this with the belief that I'm the most amazing eLearning designer in the world. In fact, I've created my fair share of crappy eLearning courses over the years!

## Here's my honest opinion: I think most eLearning sucks.

The sad reality is that most eLearning courses require our learners to sit through a disappointing experience, where information is poorly organized, the content isn't relevant, and the interactions seem contrived and without purpose. This is compounded even more when the slideshow-like presentation is interrupted with several poorly written quiz questions and cheesy animations to make it all seem "fun."

So, why is this? Why do we so often create eLearning that we ourselves wouldn't want to sit through?! Well, I'll give you my top three reasons on the next several pages.

## What Do You Think?

**What are some of the reasons you think a lot of eLearning fails?**

_____

_____

_____

**What's the cost of creating eLearning that fails?**

_____

_____

_____

# #1

## It's Not Designed For How People Learn

———

If I asked you how you learn, you might say something like "by trial and error," "by doing," or something similar. The funny thing is that most of us have a strong sense of how learning occurs. We know that learning isn't a single event but rather a process that occurs over time. However, when we're tasked with creating learning for others, whether it be an eLearning course or something else, we do a really good job throwing that logic out the window. We create a single training event, where we dump in a bunch of bullet points on a slide, add a next button, throw in a quiz, and call it "eLearning." And after that's all done, we wonder why it didn't deliver the performance results we were seeking.

In this book, we'll explore how you can create eLearning content for adults, by looking at the fundamental differences between andragogy and pedagogy. We'll also explore Malcolm Knowles' Four Principles of Adult Learning and Merrill's First Principles of Instruction.

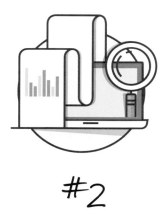

# #2

## It's Not The Right Solution For The Performance Issue

———

When your stakeholders and subject matter experts approach you to create an eLearning course, how do you respond? What questions do you ask? Do you challenge their assumptions that learning is the answer, or do you simply take the request and fulfill the order? The truth is, more often than not, our stakeholders and subject matter experts believe everything can be fixed with training. Instead, we need to validate the cause of a performance issue before we can make an informed decision as to whether eLearning (or any learning) will address it.

In this book, we'll explore how you can conduct a needs analysis to determine the cause of a performance issue, find the right answers, and design a blended training solution. We'll also explore how to work with your stakeholders and subject matter experts to plan and manage your project.

## #3

## It's Not Focused On Performance

————

When you're developing an eLearning course, you've likely been lectured about the importance of interactivity. There's this common belief that you need to make your eLearning courses interactive to maintain engagement. However, not all interactivity is created equally, nor does it have equal outcomes. You can easily add a button that reveals a bunch of bullet points when clicked. While I do believe there's a time and place for click-to-reveal interactivity, the truth is, nothing is gained from a learning and performance standpoint when it's the only type of interactivity included in your course.

In this book, we'll explore how to design and develop an eLearning course that focuses on what your learners need to do, not just on what they need to know. We'll also explore how to collect your learning content and draft a storyboard, how to develop a prototype, how to incorporate meaningful interactivity, and how to increase knowledge and skills retention by reducing cognitive load. Finally, we'll explore how to measure the effectiveness of your learning using Kirkpatrick's Four Levels of Evaluation.

---

# WHAT IS ELEARNING?

---

**In this chapter, you'll explore...**

- The different types of eLearning.

- The benefits of eLearning.

- How eLearning is designed and developed.

---

NOTES

# WHAT IS ELEARNING?

**Not all eLearning is created equally.**

What comes to mind when you think of "eLearning"? Do you imagine someone sitting behind a computer, clicking a Next button? Or maybe someone watching a video on a tablet or mobile device? Perhaps you imagine someone using a virtual reality (VR) headset? Regardless of what comes to mind, if the learning involves a digital device, it's likely a form of eLearning.

The truth is, not all eLearning is created equally. And if you're like me, when I first started in the world of eLearning, I used to think the *only* definition of eLearning was "a computer-based course, delivered via a learning management system, which involved slides, a Next button, and the occasional quiz question."

While that type of eLearning describes the eLearning this book is primarily focused on, it's important that we, as learning professionals, recognize that the term "eLearning" actually refers to a large and ever-evolving catalog of digital learning modalities.

## What Is eLearning?

So, how do I define eLearning? Well, providing a single definition of eLearning isn't easy. While you might think of eLearning as "an online, slide-based course with a Next button," the truth is, this is only one example of eLearning. Because the technology we use to access information is always evolving, there are always new examples of how it is being used to deliver learning content.

I define eLearning as any learning experience that takes place on a digital device, such as a computer, a tablet, a smartphone, or some other device.

While this definition of eLearning might seem broad, it makes the most sense when you consider all of the various ways content can be delivered digitally. For example, if you learn something by watching a YouTube video, that's an example of eLearning. If you complete an online course through a university, that's an example of eLearning. If you attend a live webinar, that's an example of eLearning. To use a cliché phrase: the possibilities are endless!

# What Are the Different Types of eLearning?

So, if there are so many different examples of eLearning, do they share any common characteristics that tie them together? Well, I'm glad you asked! The answer is, YES! While the "umbrella" of eLearning is always evolving and growing, there are a few common characteristics you can apply to the different types of eLearning.

## eLearning can be synchronous or asynchronous.

The first defining characteristic of eLearning is whether it's synchronous or asynchronous. The ability for eLearning to be group-oriented or self-paced is what truly separates eLearning from other types of traditional training modalities. Most instructor-led training is synchronous, which means all the learners are engaged in the learning event at the same time. With that being said, there are also several examples of eLearning that are synchronous, for example, a live webinar or a live, online discussion.

As for asynchronous or self-paced eLearning, this is when learners complete the learning on their own, with no set time for when the learning takes place. Examples of asynchronous eLearning include videos, interactive online courses, ongoing discussion boards, etc.

## eLearning can be interactive or passive.

The second defining characteristic of eLearning is whether it's interactive or passive. Because eLearning uses technology to deliver the learning content, the use of interactivity is often employed to enhance the learning experience. For example, the learner is given control over the navigation of a course with a menu or some other navigation buttons. While this is a simple example of how eLearning can be interactive, it's not the only example of how a learner might interact with an eLearning course. Some eLearning courses might use quiz questions to test the learners' knowledge. Other examples of interactivity include branching scenarios, where the learner makes a decision and sees (and hopefully learns from) the result of that decision. The list of how eLearning can use interactivity is nearly endless.

The list of passive eLearning examples is just as extensive. Whether it's a video, an online article, a digital infographic, or something else, any digital learning content that doesn't require the learner to interact with it can be considered passive.

# Types of eLearning

Most of the common types of eLearning can be organized into the matrix below. While this isn't a holistic list, as you think of or discover new and different types of eLearning, feel free to jot them down here.

|  | **Synchronous** | **Asynchronous** |
|---|---|---|
| **Interactive** | ■ Live webinar with polls, chat, breakout rooms, etc.<br>■ Web conference | ■ Interactive scenario<br>■ System simulation<br>■ Virtual / augmented reality<br>■ Interactive video<br>■ Online discussion board |
| **Passive** | ■ Live virtual lecture | ■ Animated explainer video<br>■ Screen recording<br>■ Podcast<br>■ Online article or blog |

# What Are the Benefits of eLearning?

While traditional, instructor-led learning is still very popular and widely used, eLearning offers a lot of benefits that just can't be matched by other training modalities. Because of this, more and more organizations have been turning to eLearning in the hopes of taking advantage of the benefits.

## eLearning can be created once and delivered multiple times, to multiple learners, in multiple locations.

**Here are just some of the benefits eLearning has to offer...**

- **eLearning can be distributed globally.**
  Because eLearning is delivered on a computer or some other internet-connected device, eLearning can be easily delivered to a large population of learners, regardless of their location.

- **eLearning is available when the learner needs it.**
  Because most eLearning doesn't require an instructor, learners can access the learning content when they need it the most.

- **eLearning can offer a consistent learning experience and message.**
  Because an eLearning course can be created once and delivered to multiple learners, eLearning can ensure that each learner receives the same learning experience and content.

- **eLearning can track learner progress.**
  Because eLearning is usually delivered through a hosting platform, like a Learning Management System (LMS), most eLearning can track and report the progress of each individual learner.

- **eLearning can save time and money.**
  Because eLearning can be created once and delivered multiple times, to multiple learners, in multiple locations, it can save time and money, when compared to traditional instructor-led training.

## How Is eLearning Designed & Developed?

So far, we've defined what eLearning is, and we've explored the different types and various benefits of eLearning; however, this doesn't explain how eLearning is created in the first place! If you're new to eLearning, I'm sure that's the question you're hoping to get answered from this book!

Well, like most things, there's isn't a single answer for how eLearning is developed. Whether you're building an eLearning course, a tree fort, or a house, it's easy to oversimplify the development (or construction) process from beginning to end.

## Designing and developing eLearning is a lot like building a house.

When you're building a house, it's easy to look at a pile of raw materials—wood beams, bricks, nails, doors, windows, flooring, etc.—and envision how they're put together to create a finished, move-in-ready home. Unfortunately, it's not that simple. Before you even hammer the first nail into a piece of wood, there are tons of questions that must be answered...

- What style of home are you building?

- How will it be laid out?

- How many bedrooms and bathrooms will it contain?

- What are the first, second, and third steps in the construction process?

- Will the owners of the house get to approve the design before you start building?

- How often will they get to review the construction process?

- Can changes be made during the construction process?

- How long will the construction process take?

**The path of eLearning development is full of twists and turns.**

The truth is, there isn't a straight line between obtaining raw content and having a finished, learner-ready eLearning course. The path is usually twisted, multifaceted, and complex.

Following a solid eLearning development process helps tame this twisted and confusing process. It provides structure and organization, not only for you, but also for your stakeholders and subject matter experts.

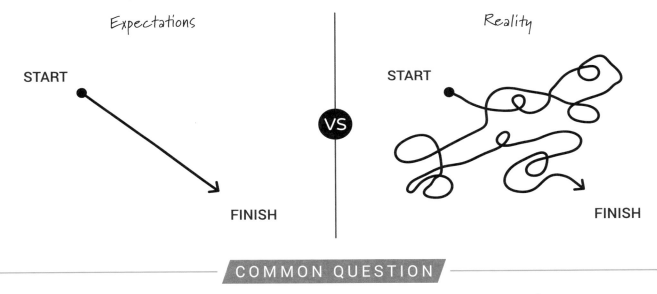

Expectations

Reality

START

START

VS

FINISH

FINISH

---

**COMMON QUESTION**

What's the difference between design and development?

While the terms "design" and "development" are often used interchangeably, they actually have very different meanings from an instructional design perspective.

- **Design** is the process of ideating and outlining a learning solution. From an eLearning perspective, this includes collecting and organizing your content into a storyboard.

- **Development** is the process of building the learning solution. From an eLearning perspective, this includes the creation of a prototype and the development of the complete, learner-ready course.

## Why Is It Important to Follow a Development Process?

When you're new to eLearning, it might seem excessive to follow a specific design and development process. You may feel inclined just to jump in and start developing your course; however, eLearning is rarely developed within a vacuum. It's likely you have stakeholders and subject matter experts who need to be involved to provide their knowledge and feedback.

## eLearning development is more complex than other types of training content.

Without following a design and development process, especially when creating eLearning, it's easy for the entire project to go off the rails. However, over the years, I've learned that any process, regardless of which one you follow, can help bring order to chaos. This is because eLearning development is far more complex than the development of other types of learning content (i.e., instructor-led training, performance support, etc.).

---

**Here's why it's important to follow a design and development process...**

### Development Time

It takes a lot longer to develop eLearning content.

**+**

### SME Experience

Most stakeholders and SMEs have little or no experience participating in the creation of eLearning.

**=**

### A Lot of Risk

You can end up wasting a lot of time.

---

# Industry-Recognized Design & Development Models

While there is no single process you must follow when designing and developing eLearning, there are several industry-recognized models, each with their own pros and cons. The two most popular models include ADDIE and SAM.

## What is ADDIE?

"ADDIE" is an acronym, which represents the five phases for developing learning content. While the ADDIE model is the most widely-known and used instructional design model, it's often criticized for its linear approach and lack of flexibility. As a result, it's often suggested that ADDIE is similar to a "waterfall" project management model, where each phase is completed sequentially.

## What is SAM?

"SAM," which is also an acronym for Successive Approximation Model, is a cyclical design and development model. Unlike the linear or waterfall approach used by ADDIE, SAM is often compared to agile project management models, in that a project will go through several, quick drafts and iterations until the ideal solution is created.

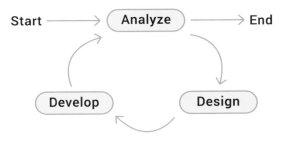

## Which Model Should You Follow?

While ADDIE and SAM are often touted as "instructional design models," in my opinion, this isn't really the case. The truth is, they are more akin to project management models, which are focused on process rather than design. As a result, there's nothing about either model which lends itself to designing and developing instructionally-sound, performance-based eLearning content.

So, which model should you use? Well, I think it totally depends on your organization, your stakeholders, the project, and your preferences. There are times when ADDIE (a waterfall approach) makes more sense, and there are times when SAM (an iterative approach) is the better choice. It always depends.

---

**Regardless of which process you decide to follow, in my experience, there are three basic principles you should always incorporate into your development process...**

**1**   *Iterative Design*   |   The process of rapidly designing, testing, and redesigning a product to achieve the best results.

**2**   *Frequent Review*   |   The process of regularly collaborating with stakeholders to obtain their feedback on the design of a given deliverable.

**3**   *Quality Design*   |   The process of achieving the highest levels of design quality, both in terms of aesthetics and content.

## Can ADDIE be iterative like SAM?

Sure! Why not? I believe it's possible to combine the best parts of ADDIE and SAM. Although ADDIE is designed as a linear process, I don't think there's any reason why you can't have multiple iterations at each stage. Regardless of which model you use, remember: you're always free to adapt it to fit your needs!

# What Do You Think?

**Which instructional design model do you think works best for you and your projects? Why?**

_____

_____

_____

**What risks or challenges might you face with your chosen design and development process?**

_____

_____

_____

**How can you adapt your process to help you overcome these risks and challenges?**

_____

_____

_____

# HOW PEOPLE LEARN

---

**In this chapter, you'll explore...**

- How people learn.

- Knowles' four principles of adult learning.

- Merrill's principles of instruction.

---

# NOTES

_____

_____

_____

_____

_____

_____

_____

_____

_____

_____

_____

_____

_____

_____

_____

_____

_____

_____

# HOW PEOPLE LEARN

**Let's start with some basics.**

At the beginning of this book, I explained the three reasons most eLearning fails, with the first one being that it's not designed for how people learn. Before we jump into how to design and develop an eLearning course, I think it's important that we explore some of the basic concepts and theories about learning in general.

While there's a lot that goes into the creation of an eLearning course, any efforts would be a total waste of time if we didn't create a course that actually results in learning. The truth is, when I was a new eLearning designer, I thought learning was simply the process of transferring information. And while that limited definition does account for a small portion of how learning occurs, it doesn't adequately describe the holistic learning process.

## How Does Learning Occur?

Let's play a little thought experiment, shall we?! Let's say you needed to learn how to bake a cake for a friend's upcoming birthday party. In the back of your mind, you know you could look up a recipe, watch a YouTube video, or even attend a class, but will you have actually learned how to bake a cake by any of those means? Probably not!

So, if you needed to master the process of baking that cake, what would you need to do? Well, you'd have to give it a try and see how it turns out! It's likely your first attempt will result in a pretty horrendous cake; however, through that failure, you may discover how you can improve your baking skills the next time. Perhaps you realize you need to be more precise when measuring your ingredients or that you need to bake the cake a bit longer. Either way, your baking skills will likely improve over time.

This is how learning occurs: trial and error. Learning is a natural part of the human condition!

## Learning isn't an event; it's a process.

So, if learning is such a natural process, why do we do such an awful job when we have to create it for others? Well, in my opinion, we try to rush the process—ignoring everything that leads up to that "ah-ha" moment we're trying to create for our learners. That's because we treat learning like an event, rather than a process.

Too often, we throw our learners into a one-hour workshop, or we sit them behind the screen of a 10-minute eLearning course, dump a ton of information on them, ask them to complete a multiple-choice quiz, and then expect them to be masters of a given topic. Of course, once that's all said and done, and it has become clear that our learners haven't learned anything, we wring our hands, wondering what went wrong. And the cycle repeats itself.

**Learning is an ecosystem of experiences.**

What we must realize is that learning doesn't just happen because we send our learners to a workshop or create an eLearning course. Learning requires trial and error. It requires desire and motivation. It requires time and patience.

To put it simply, learning is an ecosystem of experiences.

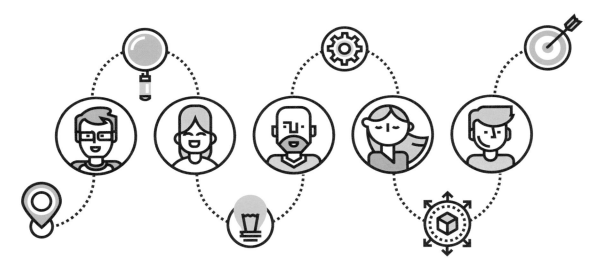

## COMMON QUESTION

### What's the difference between training and learning?

There are a lot of terms that get used interchangeably within our industry—"training" and "learning" being two of them. Here's how I separate the two...

- **Training** is any formal or informal experience or event that we create or provide for our learners. This might be an eLearning course, a job aid, a video or a workshop.

- **Learning** is the outcome or result of multiple formal or information training experiences or events.

## How Do Adults Learn?

So far, in this chapter, we've been exploring how people learn. While we can define how learning occurs in general, it's important to know that not all people learn the same way. As a result, we shouldn't treat (or train) all learners equally. This is best demonstrated through the differences between how children and adults learn.

One of the challenges many new eLearning or instructional designers face is the creation of learning experiences that are tailored specifically for the ways adults learn. Too often, we create training that mimics what you might see in a second-grade classroom, with a teacher lecturing at the front of the room.

## Adults and children learn very differently.

If you recall, at the beginning of this book, I explained how many of the learning professionals working within our industry have *no* formal training or experience when it comes to eLearning or instructional design. As a result, when someone is put into a position where they need to design a workshop or any eLearning course, it's only natural for them to mimic what they know or what they've experienced in the past. For many folks, the only experience they can rely on is the educational experience from their childhood.

While there are many different instructional design theories we could explore, I want to introduce you to the two that I think are the most important: Knowles' Principles of Adult Learning and Merrill's Principles of Instruction.

## Malcolm Knowles

Malcolm Knowles was an adult educator who was famous for his adoption of the theory of andragogy, which refers to the methods and principles used in adult education.

While andragogy was a term initially coined by the German educator Alexander Kapp in 1833, it later became popular in the United States, primarily due to the research conducted by Knowles.

Knowles suggested that andragogy, which is Greek for "man-leading," should be distinguished from the more commonly used term "pedagogy," which is Greek for "child-leading."

*Malcolm Knowles*

*Adult educator, famous for the development of the principles of andragogy.*

---

**Pedagogy vs. Andragogy...**

Pedagogy
/ˈpedəˌäjē/

The method and practice of teaching **child** learners.

Andragogy
/ˈandrəˌäjē,-gägē/

The method and practice of teaching **adult** learners.

---

## Adult vs. Child Learners

During his research, Knowles identified several characteristics that define the important differences between adult and child learners.

Specifically, these differences emphasize the need for adults to be self-directed in their learning and bring their past experiences and failures to the learning experience.

| | Adult Learners | Child Learners |
|---|---|---|
| **The Learner** | The learner self-directs and evaluates their learning experience. | The learner depends on the instructor for all learning and evaluation. |
| **Role of the Learner's Experience** | The learner brings and uses their past experiences (and mistakes) during the learning. | The learner brings and uses little past experience to the learning. |

|  | **Adult Learners** | **Child Learners** |
|---|---|---|
|  Readiness to Learn | The learner is ready to learn when any change is made to their working environment. | The learner is told what they have to learn in order to advance to the next level of mastery. |
|  Orientation to Learning | The learner wants to perform a task or solve a problem to live in a more satisfying way. | The learner is required to receive and process the prescribed subject matter. |
|  Motivation for Learning | The learner is motivated intrinsically: self-esteem, recognition, better quality of life. | The learner is motivated extrinsically: competition for grades and the consequences of failure. |

# Knowles' Four Principles of Adult Learning

As a result of his research, Knowles defined four principles or statements, which define the central tenets of how adults best learn.

---

**Knowles' Four Principles of Adult Learning are reflected in the following statements...**

 **1**

I learn when I am involved in the planning of my learning and development.

 **2**

I learn through action and reflection on ways to improve my performance.

 **3**

I learn when challenged by problems, rather than merely hearing solutions.

 **4**

I learn when the subject is relevant and is something I care about.

---

## M. David Merrill

In the early 2000s, M. David Merrill, an instructional effectiveness expert, defined a list of practical instructional design principles. Specifically, Merrill's Principles of Instruction are rooted in the creation of task-based learning, where the learner is most successful when they discover how to solve a problem that can be applied in the real world (or on the job).

While Merrill's principles help to define a successful learning experience, they don't necessarily define *how* learning occurs. Instead, the principles define how we, as instructional designers, can create experiences that promote learning.

**M. David Merrill**

*Education researcher, specializing in instructional design and technology.*

---

COMMON QUESTION

### What about the different types of learning styles?

Ugh. What about them? For years, the concept of tailoring our learning content to our learners' preferred learning style(s) (visual, auditory, written, kinesthetic) has been tossed around like a hot potato. While many learning professionals have clung onto the idea, a 2014 study by the American Psychological Association found little correlation between learning retention and method of delivery. In other words, it would be like claiming someone is an "auditory learner" because they like music or a "visual learner" because they like watching movies.

So, what should you do instead? I think the best approach is to let the content and the complexity of the task or skill being taught drive the instruction. If something is best conveyed visually, then make it visual. If it's best taught using hands-on learning, then create a tactile or experiential learning experience, etc.

It's that simple. We don't need to assign blanket assumptions onto our learner based on arbitrary ideas.

---

# Merrill's Principles of Instruction

Merrill's Principles of Instruction are intended to be applied linearly, with each principle building off the previous one.

| Principle | Description |
| --- | --- |
| 1 Demonstration | Learning is promoted when learners observe a demonstration of the skill. |
| 2 Application | Learning is promoted when learners apply their newly acquired knowledge and skill. |
| 3 Problem-Centered | Learning is promoted when learners acquire skills in the context of real-world problems. |
| 4 Activation | Learning is promoted when learners activate existing knowledge or skills. |
| 5 Integration | Learning is promoted when learners integrate their new skills into their everyday lives. |

Are these instructional design theories only for eLearning?

I'm glad you ask! Not at all! Whether it's a classroom workshop, a how-to video, a webinar or a mixture of training events, Knowles' Principles of Adult Learning and Merrill's Principles of Instruction can be applied to promote learning.

# What Do You Think?

**How could you incorporate Knowles' Principles of Adult Learning when designing eLearning?**

_____

_____

_____

**How could you incorporate Merrill's Principles of Instruction with designing eLearning?**

_____

_____

_____

**What challenges might you face when incorporating these instructional design principles?**

_____

_____

_____

# PLAN THE PROJECT

---

**In this chapter, you'll explore...**

- How to conduct a needs analysis.

- How to plan your training project.

- How to create a project plan and timeline.

# NOTES

_____
_____
_____
_____
_____
_____
_____
_____
_____
_____
_____
_____
_____
_____
_____
_____
_____
_____

# PLAN THE PROJECT

**The success of every great eLearning project starts at the very beginning.**

When you're new to eLearning, the start of any project can seem chaotic. It's easy to become overwhelmed when you're trying to collect all the information you need to design and deliver an engaging eLearning course. The process is complicated even further when you have to wrangle or hunt down stakeholders and subject matter experts to get what you need—all while you're trying to meet a tight deadline.

I remember when I started my first eLearning project. I assumed I just needed to meet with my subject matter experts, and they'd provide all the information I needed to build the course. After that, I'd then go away, create the course, and return for them to approve it. In my head, it all seemed so simple.

The reality was that my stakeholders and subject matter experts didn't have any of the information I actually needed. All they knew was that they had a performance issue with their employees, and an eLearning course was the answer.

In their minds (and mine at the time), my job was to simply fulfill the order they were making.

## When Is Training the Answer?

One of the biggest challenges we all face as learning professionals is how to respond when a stakeholder asks for training. More often than not, your stakeholders think everything can be fixed with training. As a result, the second they see a performance issue with their employees, their assumption is that training is the answer. However, this isn't always the case.

## Your stakeholders think everything can be fixed with training. They're wrong.

The truth is, how you respond when you're asked to create training has the biggest effect on whether or not any of your efforts will be successful. If you blindly accept their request, you run the risk of creating training for something that isn't a training issue in the first place!

So, when is training the answer? Well, I don't think that's the right question to be asking. Instead, we should be asking when is training *not* the answer?

## What Causes a Lack of Performance?

Before we can determine whether or not training will fix a specific performance issue, it's important to understand what causes a lack of performance in the first place.

When people don't do the things they're supposed to do, there could be any number of reasons why. Think about your own life. What's one thing you should be doing every day that you just don't? For me, it's diet and exercise. I don't always eat the right food, and I don't always exercise as often as I should. Does this mean I need more training on proper eating and exercising habits? Not at all! If I wanted to lose 30 pounds, I know that I would need to eat fewer bad foods and exercise more often. It's not a lack of knowledge or skill that's preventing me from losing weight. It's that I don't have (or I don't think I have) enough time in my day.

This same concept applies to people at work. If your stakeholders have folks who aren't performing a specific task, is it possible the cause has nothing to do with a lack of knowledge or training? Of course, it does, and it's our job to uncover those issues so that we can identify and recommend the right solution.

**Most performance issues are caused by a mixture of the following...**

### Lack of Knowledge

The learner doesn't know how to perform a task. For example, a salesperson doesn't know the features and benefits of a product to sell it to a customer.

### Lack of Skill

The learner doesn't have the skill to perform a desired task at the desired level of proficiency. For example, a salesperson struggles to overcome the objections of a potential customer.

### Lack of Motivation

The learner isn't motivated to perform the task. For example, a salesperson is commissioned higher for selling some products versus others.

### Lack of Resources

The learner lacks the resources necessary to perform the desired task. For example, the systems the salesperson are required to use are slower and take longer than the desired time of completion.

## What performance issues can training actually fix?

That's the golden question! Obviously, we can create training that increases knowledge or improves someone's skill. But what about a lack of motivation or resources? Can training fix these as well? The quick answer is no, but I think there are some instances when training can help.

While training by itself won't magically motivate your learners or provide them the resources they need, training can help uncover the benefits your learners might gain from applying their existing knowledge or skills (if they exists). Training can also help expose your learners to performance support resources that can help improve the use of their existing knowledge or skills.

With that being said, I don't think that's enough of a justification alone for creating training. There are far more effective and efficient methods for delivering that information.

# What Do You Think?

**What are some examples within your organization (or a past organization) where training *would not* have had the desired effect on performance? Why?**

_____

_____

_____

**For those examples above, what would have been the more appropriate solution, besides training?**

_____

_____

_____

# Conduct a Needs Analysis

On the last few pages, we explored why training isn't always the answer to the performance issues your learners might be exhibiting. We also explored some of the contributing factors that can cause a performance issue.

But how can you actually validate the cause of a performance issue and determine the right solution? Well, this is where a needs analysis can help!

**What is a needs analysis?**

Whether you call it a "needs analysis," a "training needs assessment," a "performance assessment," or something else, a needs analysis is simply the process of evaluating a performance issue to determine the root cause and offer one or more solutions.

That's pretty simple, right?! Then, why do we make it so much harder for ourselves, and why is it so important that we conduct a needs analysis in the first place?!

Well, let's turn the page and find out why.

### Why should you conduct a needs analysis?

When I was new to eLearning, I used to cringe when I heard someone suggest that I should conduct a needs analysis. To be honest, I used to think it was a massive waste of time. I wasn't sure what I was supposed to do or which questions I was supposed to ask. The truth is, I was intimidated by the process. However, over the years, I've since realized—and can happily admit—I was totally wrong! What I learned is that if you don't know why a performance issue exists, you run the risk of creating a training solution for a non-training problem—something that's a total waste of everyone's time!

If you don't know why a performance issue exists, you run the risk of creating a training solution for a non-training problem.

Too often, when we act as order takers for our stakeholders and start working on a training project, it's only until we're nearly done developing the training that we realize that it's not the right solution. This realization comes from the context that we've gained through the development of the training, and it's this type of information that a needs analysis can help us obtain before we start developing any kind of training solutions.

## How do you conduct a needs analysis?

While conducting a needs analysis might seem like some arduous process, it's actually pretty straightforward. Yes, it might require you to crunch some numbers and analyze data; however, it's more about understanding the issue so that you can make an informed recommendation. A proper needs analysis can help you pinpoint and tailor your learning content on the actual performance needs of your learners, rather than knowledge alone.

---

**Most needs analyses seek to answer three basic questions...**

### What are people doing?

Answer this question to determine the *current level* of performance.

### What do you want people doing?

Answer this question to determine the *desired level* of performance.

### Why aren't people doing it?

Answer this question to determine the *cause* of performance.

---

## What Do You Think?

When you're asked to create training within your organization, do you start by conducting a needs analysis? If so, what does your process look like? If not, why not?

_____

_____

_____

When conducting a needs analysis, how you go about collecting the information you need in order to answer the three questions on the previous page depends on your organization, the performance issue(s) you're analyzing, and much more.

It's important not to rely on any single piece of data (i.e., the opinions of your stakeholders and subject matter experts) when you're working to determine the cause of a performance issue. The more you can learn about the performance issue and why it's happening, the more you'll be prepared to make an informed decision about how to address it.

**Here are some ways to collect information for your needs analysis...**

| | |
|---|---|
| Talk to Your Stakeholders | Talk to your stakeholders and subject matter experts to see why they believe the performance issue exists. While this is a good place to start, don't rely 100% on what they have to say. Remember, they think everything can be fixed with training. |
| Review Any Data | Review any available data or key performance indicators (KPIs), which can be used to determine the cause of the performance issue. This same data can be used to evaluate the effectiveness of any training or non-training solutions you implement. |
| Observe Your Learners | Observe your learners to see what they are and aren't doing as it relates to the performance issue. This can also help you determine how much of a gap exists between the current and desired behaviors. |
| Talk to Your Learners | Talk to your learners and see what they have to say about why they aren't performing as expected. This will help you quickly identify whether or not there's a gap in knowledge or skill. |
| Review Best Practices | Review any best practices (if available) related to the performance issue you're analyzing. You may discover there is unclear or conflicting information regarding the tasks or behaviors your analyzing. |

# Recommend a Solution

Once you've completed a needs analysis, you should be able to make informed recommendations on possible solutions for addressing the performance issues identified. Remember, not all recommendations will involve a training solution. Sometimes, you'll make recommendations that involve procedural or cultural changes within your organization.

The goal of a needs analysis isn't to determine what training is needed. The goal is to determine how to address a performance issue.

Depending on your organization, your stakeholders, and subject matter experts, you can expect some pushback on your non-training recommendations. However, the more you can reinforce your recommendations with data and evidence, the more likely they'll be adopted.

## PRO TIP

When you're talking with your stakeholders and subject matter experts, ask questions and focus your discussion on what you want your learners to be *doing* rather than knowing.

## Conduct a Kickoff Meeting

The success of most eLearning projects hinges on the relationships you create and maintain with your stakeholders, subject matter experts, and anyone else who is contributing to the development of the course. In my experience, one of the best ways to start these relationships off on the right foot is to conduct a project kickoff meeting.

Although the purpose of an eLearning project kickoff meeting might seem self-explanatory, it's not always obvious what should occur during this initial meeting. Who should you invite? What questions should you ask? What decisions must you make?

### What is a project kickoff meeting?

An eLearning project kickoff meeting is pretty simple but very important. It's a chance to gather everyone involved in the project to discuss the eLearning course you're planning to build and gain agreement on their involvement in the project.

At this very early stage, you may or may not know the full scope of the project or even what content needs to be included in the course. Sometimes, you'll need to answer these questions as part of your kickoff meeting, and other times, you'll conduct your kickoff meeting with these questions clearly answered. The point is: every kickoff meeting is a little different.

## When should I conduct a kickoff meeting?

When you conduct your kickoff meeting (and what you discuss) largely depends on where you're at in the process. Have you conducted a needs analysis? Are you ready to start designing and developing your eLearning course?

I recommend conducting a kickoff meeting when...

| A request for training is made. | You're ready to design training. |
|---|---|
| **Focuses On...** | **Focuses On...** |
| ■ Stakeholders<br>■ Business Goals<br>■ Performance Gaps | ■ Subject Matter Experts<br>■ Learning Objectives<br>■ Learning Content |
| **Results In...** | **Results In...** |
| ■ The Completion of a Needs Analysis | ■ The Creation of Training |

# What Do You Think?

**Do you typically conduct a kickoff meeting when starting a new project? If so, at what point during the process do you usually schedule it?**

_____

_____

_____

## Invite the Right People

Facilitating a successful eLearning project kickoff meeting starts by inviting the right people. The kickoff meeting is one of the few opportunities you'll get to have everyone in the same room (or on the same conference line). You don't want to waste this opportunity! Inviting the right people to your kickoff meeting lets you ask questions, answer questions, collect content, and set expectations.

## You and your subject matter experts need each other! They possess the information you need to solve their problem.

While you definitely want to involve all of the major "players" involved in the project (e.g., your stakeholders, subject matter experts, and other reviewers), you want to avoid inviting more people than necessary. Only those individuals who are actually necessary to the development, delivery, and approval of the course should be invited. If you find yourself with your stakeholders' boss's boss, you might have too many people.

The cost of involving too many people in the planning of your project will likely result in a project that is wildly out of scope.

### COMMON QUESTION

### What's the difference between a stakeholder and subject matter expert?

To be 100% honest, I sometimes use these two terms interchangeably; however, there is an important difference between the two.

- A **stakeholder** is someone who has a vested interest in the project and the outcomes of the project. This might be a higher-level executive or someone else closely related to the topic area of the project. Stakeholders are also sometimes referred to as "project sponsors."

- A **subject matter expert**, or SME, is someone who has deep operational, functional, and applicable knowledge of the topic being addressed in the project.

**Here's who you should invite to your kickoff meeting...**

### Yourself

This one might seem obvious, but I have to say it nonetheless. The eLearning project kickoff meeting is your meeting. You are responsible for scheduling it, facilitating it, and inviting the right people to the meeting.

### Stakeholders

It's important to include certain individuals, even if they aren't directly involved in the project. This includes your project stakeholders. Being involved gives these folks an opportunity to ask questions and see the direction the project is heading.

### Subject Matter Experts

Your subject matter experts are the ones you'll be working the closest with during the eLearning development process. The truth is, you and your subject matter experts need each other! They possess the information you need to solve their problem.

### Other Designers

Finally, you'll want to invite any other designers or developers working on the project. Although this may not be the case with every project, anyone participating in the development of the course should be present.

What if one of my stakeholders or SMEs doesn't show up to the kickoff meeting?

Reschedule the meeting. The kickoff meeting is your opportunity to set and manage expectations while everyone is in the same room *before* you dive head-first into the project. If one of your stakeholders is unable to dedicate the time for a kickoff meeting, don't hold your breath on them being timely with feedback or anything else. This might also be a sign they are not the right person to contribute to the project.

# What Do You Think?

**Who do you typically invite to your kickoff meetings?**

_____

_____

_____

**What topics do you typically discuss during your kickoff meetings?**

_____

_____

_____

**What questions do you typically ask during your kickoff meeting?**

_____

_____

_____

## Ask the Right Questions

Your kickoff meeting is an opportunity to ask questions, get answers, and make sure you're on the same page as your stakeholders. While a needs analysis may answer many of your questions related to the learning needs and desired outcomes of the course, it's still a good idea to get a sense of what your stakeholders are thinking.

Additionally, how your stakeholders and subject matter experts respond to your questions can also help you uncover misaligned expectations that you'll want to address during the kickoff meeting. For example, if they expect you to design and deliver the finished course within a week, this might be something you should address sooner than later.

Remember, you need your stakeholders and subject matter experts. They possess the information you need to solve their problem. However, they won't hand you all the information you need on a silver platter—you have to dig!

**PRO TIP**

Don't expect your stakeholders to be able to answer all the questions on the following pages. You will need to answer some of these questions for yourself. Don't interrogate your stakeholders! Incorporate these questions into your normal conversations.

## Questions for Project Scope...

| | |
|---|---|
| *When does this eLearning course need to be available?* | Ask this question to determine the target date for when the course development is to be completed and when the course should be available to learners. This can help you build your eLearning project timeline. |
| *How long do you think this eLearning course should be?* | Ask this question to determine how much learning content your SME is expecting you to deliver and how long it will take to develop. This can help you scope the total project and estimate the amount of time you need to budget for development. |
| *Who are the target learners for this course?* | Ask this question to determine the audience for the course. This can help you better understand the specific needs of this audience. |

# What Do You Think?

**What other questions would you ask regarding the project scope?**

_____

_____

_____

_____

_____

**Questions for Desired Outcomes...**

What goals or metrics can be most affected by this course?

Ask this question to determine how you can correlate this course to a measurable goal. This can help you design content that is focused on positively affecting those goals or metrics.

What behaviors have the most positive effect on these goals or metrics?

Ask this question to determine the behaviors that have the most positive impact on the stated goal(s). This can help you design interactions that emulate and encourage these behaviors.

How much of an effect would you like this course to have on these goals or metrics?

Ask this question to determine how much your SME expects the course to affect their goal(s). This can help you put greater emphasis on ensuring the course focuses on the right information and behaviors.

# What Do You Think?

**What other questions would you ask regarding the desired outcomes?**

_____

_____

_____

_____

_____

## Questions for Course Content...

**What do learners need to know to perform the desired behaviors?**

Ask this question to determine what knowledge is required to perform the desired behaviors. This can help you focus on information that is related to behaviors, rather than nice-to-know information.

**What existing resources, best practices, or training are currently available on this topic?**

Ask this question to determine what content can be referenced or used for the development of the course. This can help you save time by not recreating existing content.

**How effective or ineffective is the existing content or training?**

Ask this question to determine what is and is not working with the existing resources or training. This can help ensure your course focuses on what's most effective.

# What Do You Think?

**What other questions would you ask regarding course content?**

_____
_____
_____
_____
_____

**Questions for Course Development...**

| | |
|---|---|
| Have you ever participated in the development of an eLearning course? | Ask this question to determine the experience your SME has with the eLearning development process. This can help you educate your SME on the development process. |
| How would you describe what effective and ineffective eLearning looks like? | Ask this question to determine how your SME views good and bad eLearning. This can help you identify any misconceptions your SME has regarding eLearning. |
| Who needs to review this course and how much time is required to provide feedback? | Ask this question to determine who your course reviewers are and how much time is needed to provide edits. This can help you make sure the right people are included in the development and review process. |

# What Do You Think?

**What other questions would you ask regarding course development?**

_____

_____

_____

_____

_____

**Questions for Course Delivery...**

| | |
|---|---|
| How will this course be communicated to learners? | Ask this question to determine who is responsible for ensuring the course is made available to learners. This will help you make sure the course is implemented properly. |
| Do learners need to complete this course by a certain date? If so, why? | Ask this question to determine what expectations your SME has for learner completion and why. This can help you plan for course delivery and implementation. |
| Who is responsible for ensuring learners complete the course by the stated date? | Ask this question to determine who is responsible for ensuring learners complete the course by the stated date. This can help you make sure everyone understands their responsibilities. |

# What Do You Think?

**What other questions would you ask regarding course delivery?**

_____

_____

_____

_____

_____

## Align on Expectations

Planning your eLearning project during the kickoff meeting is mostly about managing and aligning expectations. While you might want to get into the "nitty gritty" of the content or learning outcomes of your course, it's important to spend time ensuring you and your stakeholders have a clear understanding of the outcomes of the project.

Remember, while your stakeholders and subject matter experts might know a lot about the content of what needs to be taught, they aren't experts in eLearning course development. With that said, you should plan to dedicate some time during the kickoff meeting to help your stakeholders understand the eLearning development process, what makes a good eLearning course, their role in the development and review process, and of course, what will actually be delivered or created at the end of the project.

### Outline the eLearning development process.

It's easy to assume your stakeholders and subject matter experts understand the overall eLearning development or project management process. Although your subject matter experts may have been involved in many different projects, that's no guarantee that they'll understand things like learning objectives, storyboards, prototypes, or review cycles.

During your kickoff meeting, take the time to educate them on the eLearning development process. Explain what they should expect during each phase of the process and explain any terms they may not understand.

---
PRO TIP
---

Analogies are a great way to help your stakeholders understand the development process. I like to compare the creation of an eLearning course to the construction of a house, with the storyboard as the blueprint, the prototype as the 3D rendering, and development as the construction of the house.

I like this analogy when explaining the importance of making any changes during the storyboarding process, rather than waiting until full development. Just like building a house, any changes can be made to a blueprint; however, once construction starts, if you want to move the kitchen, it might mean redesigning and rebuilding the entire house.

---

**Help them understand good eLearning design.**

After working in the field of eLearning for many years, it's easy to forget that not everyone knows what good eLearning looks like! This is especially true when you're working with stakeholders. More often than not, stakeholders and subject matter experts aren't learning professionals.

Never make the mistake of assuming stakeholders can recognize good eLearning. While they might have a vague idea about the concepts of computer-based training, their knowledge might be 5, 10, or 15 years out of date. When you first meet with your subject matter experts, make a point to educate them about the qualities of good eLearning design. Show them examples of your work and encourage them to ask questions. Don't end that meeting until you're on the same page!

## COMMON QUESTION

### What makes good eLearning?

I've always believed that a good eLearning course is made of these four components...

- **Graphic Design:** We eat with our eyes first, and we learn with our eyes first. An eLearning course should be visually engaging, using good graphic design techniques.

- **Visual Communications:** eLearning is a tool for visual communications. Rather than putting a bunch of words on the screen, help your learners see what you're saying by using images, icons, and animations to bring your content to life.

- **User Interface Design:** If your eLearning course is confusing to navigate, full of functional glitches, or anything else that impedes the learning experience, your learners will spend more time learning how to navigate the course, rather than absorbing the actual learning content.

- **Instructional Design:** Finally, all the items above are pointless if the eLearning course isn't designed using solid instructional design techniques. Your eLearning course should support improved performance in your learners rather than just knowledge retention.

**Explain their role in the development and review process.**

Not all stakeholders are the same: some like to be heavily involved, and others barely have time to respond to your emails. Either way, it's your job to clarify what role they play in the eLearning development process. As I mentioned earlier, you and your subject matter experts need each other. They possess the information you need to solve their problem. Your job is to get it from them (hopefully without being too much of a pest).

When working with stakeholders, don't make the mistake of letting them make assumptions. When you fail to set expectations with stakeholders, you run the risk of losing control of the project or finding they have disengaged altogether. Make sure to explain to your stakeholders and subject matter experts what you need from them throughout the process. Creating an eLearning project plan is an excellent way to establish accountability and ensure your subject matter experts play an active role throughout the project.

# What Do You Think?

**What other expectations do you need to align on with your stakeholders and SMEs?**

_____

_____

_____

**What strategies or analogies can you use to help your stakeholders and SMEs understand their role?**

_____

_____

_____

## Create a Project Plan

It's easy to walk away from your initial eLearning project kickoff meeting assuming everyone is on the same page and has the same expectations. However, this is rarely the case.

While much of the kickoff meeting is spent discussing the desired outcomes of the course, collecting content, and aligning expectations, all the information and decisions made during the meeting can easily remain ambiguous once everyone walks away. This is where scope creep can start to "creep" in. One way to avoid this and ensure you're aligned with the expectations of your stakeholders is to create a project plan and timeline.

### What is a project plan?

An eLearning project plan is a simple document designed to outline all the important details related to the project. I like to think of a project plan as a contract between you and your stakeholders and subject matter experts.

Documenting the details and deliverables of a project helps to solidify everything that was agreed upon during the kickoff meeting. A project plan also helps to maintain accountability throughout the development process and ensure everyone involved understands their responsibilities.

### COMMON QUESTION

#### What is scope creep?

"Scope creep" is a project management term that refers to the unexpected, uncontrollable, or continuous change in the scope of the overall project after it has begun. Scope creep is usually the result of poor stakeholder management, poor communication, and misaligned expectations. When scope creep runs amok, it can put the entire project at risk, causing delays and the inclusion of unnecessary, nice-to-know content or features within an eLearning course.

## What's included in a project plan?

Project plans come in all sorts of shapes and sizes—with there being no single method for creating or formatting a project plan or what information to include in it. What's important is that you include the right information you need in order to gain agreement and accountability with your stakeholders and subject matter experts.

Your plan should include enough information to give anyone a strong sense of what the project aims to achieve and the deliverables that will result from the project.

# PROJECT PLAN

### PROJECT INFORMATION

| | |
|---|---|
| Project Title | Consultative Sales 101 |
| Project Description | This project has been initiated to create a self-paced eLearning course and supplemental materials, helping our sales associates adopt our new consultative sales program. |

### ROLES & RESPONSIBILITIES

| | |
|---|---|
| eLearning Designer | Tim Slade, Instructional Designer |
| Project Stakeholder(s) | Kate Morrison, VP of Customer Experience |
| Subject Matter Expert(s) | Tripp Mckay, North America Sales Manager |
| | Rosalee Melvin, Europe Sales Manager |
| Other Contributors | Aidyn Cody, LMS Administrator |

### PROJECT DELIVERABLES

| | |
|---|---|
| Target Audience | Customer Service Associates |
| Learning Objectives | After completing this course, learners will be able to... |
| | • Apply the five-step consultative framework to engage potential customers. <br> • Identify customer needs by asking open-ended qualifying questions. <br> • Present tailored product and service solutions to qualified customers. |
| Description of Deliverables | The scope of this project includes the following deliverables... |
| | • Three-week email campaign, announcing the launch of the new consultative sales framework. <br> • 10-minute eLearning course, covering the five-step consultative framework. <br> • One-page job aid, listing example open-ended qualifying questions. <br> • One-hour workshop, allowing for learners to practice the consultative steps and presenting solutions. |

### IMPLEMENTATION & MEASUREMENT

| | |
|---|---|
| Project Risks / Constraints | Availability of subject matter experts. |
| Measurement(s) of Success | 10% increase in new revenue sales by Q3. <br> 15% increase in customer satisfaction scores by Q3. |
| Implementation | Email Campaign: Scheduled and sent by communications team. <br> eLearning Course: Hosted within the learning management system. <br> Job Aid: Published to sales hub intranet. <br> Workshop: Scheduled within the learning management system. |

# PROJECT PLAN

## PROJECT INFORMATION

| | |
|---|---|
| **Project Title** | Consultative Sales 101 |
| **Project Description** | This project has been initiated to create a self-paced eLearning course and supplemental materials, helping our sales associates adopt our new consultative sales program. |

| | |
|---|---|
| eLearning Designer | Tim Slade, Instructional Designer |
| Project Stakeholder(s) | Kate Morrison, VP of Customer Experience |
| Subject Matter Expert(s) | Tripp Mckay, North America Sales Manager |
| | Rosalee Melvin, Europe Sales Manager |
| Other Contributors | Aidyn Cody, LMS Administrator |

### PROJECT DELIVERABLES

| | |
|---|---|
| Target Audience | Customer Service Associates |
| Learning Objectives | After completing this course, learners will be able to… |

- Apply the five-step consultative framework to engage potential customers.
- Identify customer needs by asking open-ended qualifying questions.
- Present tailored product and service solutions to qualified customers.

| | |
|---|---|
| Description of Deliverables | The scope of this project includes the following deliverables… |

- Three-week email campaign, announcing the launch of the new consultative sales framework.
- 10-minute eLearning course, covering the five-step consultative framework.
- One-page job aid, listing example open-ended qualifying questions.
- One-hour workshop, allowing for learners to practice the consultative steps and presenting solutions.

### IMPLEMENTATION & MEASUREMENT

| | |
|---|---|
| Project Risks / Constraints | Availability of subject matter experts. |
| Measurement(s) of Success | 10% increase in new revenue sales by Q3. |
| | 15% increase in customer satisfaction scores by Q3. |
| Implementation | Email Campaign: Scheduled and sent by communications team. |
| | eLearning Course: Hosted within the learning management system. |
| | Job Aid: Published to sales hub intranet. |
| | Workshop: Scheduled within the learning management system. |

**Detail the Basic Project Information...**

Project Title

Use this space to define the title of the project or the course.

Project Description

Use this space to outline a description of the project, including a high-level overview of its history, goals, and deliverables.

# What Do You Think?

**What other project information might you want to document in your project plan?**

_____

_____

_____

_____

_____

# PROJECT PLAN

## PROJECT INFORMATION

Project Title
Consultative Sales 101

Project Description
This project has been initiated to create a self-paced eLearning course and supplemental materials, helping our sales associates

# ROLES & RESPONSIBILITIES

| | |
|---|---|
| eLearning Designer | Tim Slade, Instructional Designer |
| Project Stakeholder(s) | Kate Morrison, VP of Customer Experience |
| Subject Matter Expert(s) | Tripp Mckay, North America Sales Manager |
| | Rosalee Melvin, Europe Sales Manager |
| Other Contributors | Aidyn Cody, LMS Administrator |

Learning Objectives
After completing this course, learners will be able to...

- Apply the five-step consultative framework to engage potential customers.
- Identify customer needs by asking open-ended qualifying questions.
- Present tailored product and service solutions to qualified customers.

Description of Deliverables
The scope of this project includes the following deliverables...

- Three-week email campaign, announcing the launch of the new consultative sales framework.
- 10-minute eLearning course, covering the five-step consultative framework.
- One-page job aid, listing example open-ended qualifying questions.
- One-hour workshop, allowing for learners to practice the consultative steps and presenting solutions.

## IMPLEMENTATION & MEASUREMENT

Project Risks / Constraints
Availability of subject matter experts.

Measurement(s) of Success
10% increase in new revenue sales by Q3.
15% increase in customer satisfaction scores by Q3.

Implementation
Email Campaign: Scheduled and sent by communications team.
eLearning Course: Hosted within the learning management system.
Job Aid: Published to sales hub intranet.
Workshop: Scheduled within the learning management system.

**Document Roles & Responsibilities...**

eLearning Designer | Use this space to document the primary designer / developer for the project, even if it's just yourself.

Project Stakeholder(s) | Use this space to document your project stakeholders and sponsors.

Subject Matter Expert(s) | Use this space to document the subject matter experts who will provide their expertise in the development of the course.

Other Contributors | Use this space to document anyone else contributing to the project (i.e., other developers, LMS admins, etc.).

# What Do You Think?

**What other roles and responsibilities might you want to document in your project plan?**

_____

_____

_____

_____

_____

# PROJECT PLAN

PROJECT INFORMATION

Project Title                          Consultative Sales 101

Project Description                    This project has been initiated to create a self-paced eLearning
                                       course and supplemental materials, helping our sales associates
                                       adopt our new consultative sales program.

ROLES & RESPONSIBILITIES

eLearning Designer                     Tim Slade, Instructional Designer

## PROJECT DELIVERABLES

**Target Audience**            Customer Service Associates

**Learning Objectives**        After completing this course, learners will be able to...

- Apply the five-step consultative framework to engage potential customers.
- Identify customer needs by asking open-ended qualifying questions.
- Present tailored product and service solutions to qualified customers.

**Description of Deliverables**        The scope of this project includes the following deliverables...

- Three-week email campaign, announcing the launch of the new consultative sales framework.
- 10-minute eLearning course, covering the five-step consultative framework.
- One-page job aid, listing example open-ended qualifying questions.
- One-hour workshop, allowing for learners to practice the consultative steps and presenting solutions.

eLearning Course: Hosted within the learning management system.
Job Aid: Published to sales hub intranet.
Workshop: Scheduled within the learning management system.

**Define the Deliverables of the Project...**

| | |
|---|---|
| Target Audience | Use this space to provide a description of the target audience of the course. |
| Learning Objectives | Use this space to list your learning and / or performance objectives. |
| Description of Deliverables | Use this space to define each of the deliverables that will result from the project. |

# What Do You Think?

**What other deliverables might you want to document in your project plan?**

_____

_____

_____

_____

_____

# PROJECT PLAN

## PROJECT INFORMATION

| | |
|---|---|
| Project Title | Consultative Sales 101 |
| Project Description | This project has been initiated to create a self-paced eLearning course and supplemental materials, helping our sales associates adopt our new consultative sales program. |

## ROLES & RESPONSIBILITIES

| | |
|---|---|
| eLearning Designer | Tim Slade, Instructional Designer |
| Project Stakeholder(s) | Kate Morrison, VP of Customer Experience |
| Subject Matter Expert(s) | Tripp Mckay, North America Sales Manager |
| | Rosalee Melvin, Europe Sales Manager |
| Other Contributors | Aidyn Cody, LMS Administrator |

## PROJECT DELIVERABLES

| | |
|---|---|
| Target Audience | Customer Service Associates |
| Learning Objectives | After completing this course, learners will be able to... |

- Apply the five-step consultative framework to engage potential customers
- Identify customer needs by asking open-ended qualifying questions
- Present tailored product and service solutions to qualified customers

| | |
|---|---|
| Description of Deliverables | The scope of this project includes the following deliverables... |

- Three-week email campaign, announcing the

## IMPLEMENTATION & MEASUREMENT

| | |
|---|---|
| **Project Risks / Constraints** | Availability of subject matter experts. |
| **Measurement(s) of Success** | 10% increase in new revenue sales by Q3. 15% increase in customer satisfaction scores by Q3. |
| **Implementation** | Email Campaign: Scheduled and sent by communications team. eLearning Course: Hosted within the learning management system. Job Aid: Published to sales hub intranet. Workshop: Scheduled within the learning management system. |

**Outline the Plans for Implementation & Measurement...**

| | |
|---|---|
| Project Risks / Constraints | Use this space to outline any risks or constraints that may prevent the successful delivery and completion of the project. |
| Measurement(s) of Success | Use this space to define how the success of the course will be measured. This may be a specific metric or something similar. |
| Implementation | Use this space to outline how the course will be implemented. For example, if the course will be distributed and tracked via a Learning Management System (LMS). |

# What Do You Think?

**What other implementation and measurement information might you want to document in your project plan?**

_____

_____

_____

_____

## Draft a Project Timeline

The progression of an eLearning project, or any learning project, is dependent on multiple people coming together to work towards a common goal. While your project plan will help you align with your stakeholders and subject matter experts on the deliverables of the project, it's the project timeline that will help ensure everyone contributes to the successful delivery of those deliverables.

A project timeline is something you should create alongside your project plan. While I usually include a project timeline within the project plan itself, for the sake of this book and the importance of a timeline in the eLearning development process, I am discussing it separately.

### Why create a project timeline?

Any project, eLearning or otherwise, should have a timeline associated with it. Just like your project plan, a timeline is yet another tool you can use to set expectations with your stakeholders. This is especially important when your stakeholders and subject matter experts have responsibilities or contributions to the project itself.

**Creating a project timeline will help you...**

Define when the project will come to an end and when the eLearning course is ready for implementation.

Establish accountability with your stakeholders regarding what they are responsible for delivering and when they are responsible for delivering it.

Provide a holistic sense of the project scope, letting contributors see all of the tasks needed to deliver the requested eLearning course.

## What's included in a project timeline?

While project timelines come in many different shapes and sizes, it's my opinion that a project timeline should, at the very least...

- Define each milestone or deliverable in the project.

- Define who is responsible for each milestone or deliverable.

- Define when each milestone or deliverable is expected to be completed.

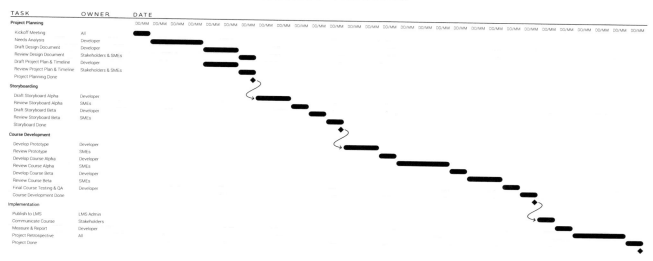

PROJECT TIMELINE

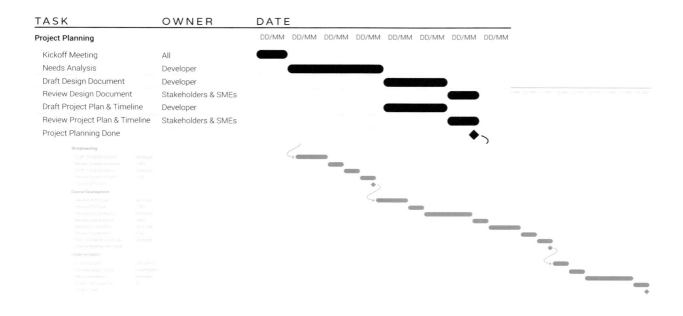

| TASK | OWNER | DATE | | | | | | | |
|---|---|---|---|---|---|---|---|---|---|
| | | DD/MM | DD/MM | DD/MM | DD/MM | DD/MM | DD/MM | DD/MM | DD/MM |
| **Project Planning** | | | | | | | | | |
| Kickoff Meeting | All | | | | | | | | |
| Needs Analysis | Developer | | | | | | | | |
| Draft Design Document | Developer | | | | | | | | |
| Review Design Document | Stakeholders & SMEs | | | | | | | | |
| Draft Project Plan & Timeline | Developer | | | | | | | | |
| Review Project Plan & Timeline | Stakeholders & SMEs | | | | | | | | |
| Project Planning Done | | | | | | | | | |

**Start by listing all of the tasks, owners and due dates related to planning the project.**

This includes the time spent...

- Conducting your kickoff meeting.

- Conducting a needs analysis.

- Drafting a design document.

- Reviewing / approving the design document with your stakeholders and SMEs.

- Drafting a project plan and timeline.

- Reviewing / approving the project plan and timeline with your stakeholders and SMEs.

# What Do You Think?

**What other project planning tasks might you want to list in your timeline?**

_____

_____

_____

_____

_____

## PROJECT TIMELINE

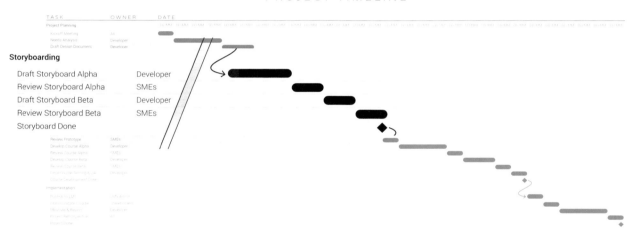

| TASK | OWNER | DATE |
|---|---|---|
| **Project Planning** | | |
| Kickoff Meeting | All | |
| Needs Analysis | Developer | |
| Draft Design Documents | Developer | |

### Storyboarding

| | | |
|---|---|---|
| Draft Storyboard Alpha | Developer | |
| Review Storyboard Alpha | SMEs | |
| Draft Storyboard Beta | Developer | |
| Review Storyboard Beta | SMEs | |
| Storyboard Done | | |

| | | |
|---|---|---|
| Review Prototype | SMEs | |
| Develop Course Alpha | Developer | |
| Review Course Alpha | SMEs | |
| Develop Course Beta | Developer | |
| Review Course Beta | SMEs | |
| Finish Course Technical Dev | Developer | |
| Course Development Done | | |
| **Implementation** | | |
| Publish to LMS | LMS Admin | |
| Communicate Course | Developer | |
| Evaluate & Revise | Developer | |
| Project Retrospective | All | |
| Project Done | | |

**Next, list all of the tasks, owners and due dates related to drafting a storyboard.**

This includes the time spent...

- Drafting the storyboard alpha (first draft).

- Reviewing and approving the storyboard alpha with your stakeholders and SMEs.

- Drafting the storyboard beta (second draft).

- Reviewing / approving the storyboard beta with your stakeholders and SMEs.

# What Do You Think?

**What other storyboarding tasks might you want to list in your timeline?**

_____

_____

_____

_____

# PROJECT TIMELINE

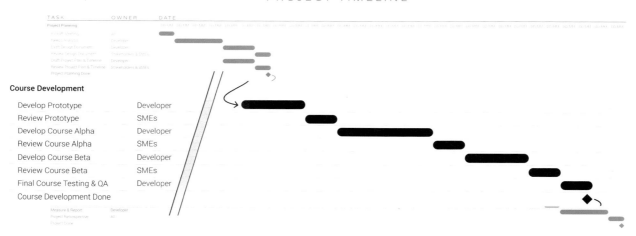

| TASK | OWNER | DATE |
|---|---|---|
| **Project Planning** | | |
| Kickoff Meeting | All | |
| Needs Analysis | Developer | |
| Draft Design Document | Developer | |
| Review Design Document | Stakeholders & SMEs | |
| Draft Project Plan & Timeline | Developer | |
| Review Project Plan & Timeline | Stakeholders & SMEs | |
| Project Planning Done | | |

## Course Development

| Develop Prototype | Developer |
|---|---|
| Review Prototype | SMEs |
| Develop Course Alpha | Developer |
| Review Course Alpha | SMEs |
| Develop Course Beta | Developer |
| Review Course Beta | SMEs |
| Final Course Testing & QA | Developer |
| Course Development Done | |

| Measure & Report | Developer |
|---|---|
| Project Retrospective | All |
| Project Done | |

**Next, list all of the tasks, owners and due dates related to developing the course.**

This includes the time spent...

- Developing a course prototype.

- Reviewing and approving the course prototype with your stakeholders and SMEs.

- Developing the course alpha (first draft).

- Reviewing / approving the storyboard alpha with your stakeholders and SMEs.

- Developing the course beta (second draft).

- Testing and conducting a quality assurance (QA) check of the final course.

# What Do You Think?

**What other course development tasks might you want to list in your timeline?**

_____
_____
_____
_____
_____

# PROJECT TIMELINE

| TASK | OWNER | DATE |
| --- | --- | --- |
| **Project Planning** | | |
| Kick-Off Meeting | All | |
| Needs Analysis | Developer | |
| Draft Design Document | Developer | |
| Review Design Document | Stakeholders & SMEs | |
| Draft Project Plan & Timeline | Developer | |
| Review Project Plan & Timeline | Stakeholders & SMEs | |
| Project Planning Done | | |
| **Storyboarding** | | |
| Draft Storyboard Alpha | Developer | |
| Review Storyboard Alpha | SMEs | |
| Draft Storyboard Beta | Developer | |
| Review Storyboard Beta | SMEs | |
| Storyboard Done | | |
| **Course Development** | | |
| Develop Prototype | Developer | |
| Review Prototype | SMEs | |
| Develop Course Alpha | Developer | |
| Review Course Alpha | SMEs | |
| Develop Course Beta | Developer | |
| Review Course Beta | SMEs | |
| **Implementation** | | |
| Publish to LMS | LMS Admin | |
| Communicate Course | Stakeholders | |
| Measure & Report | Developer | |
| Project Retrospective | All | |
| Project Done | | |

**Finally, list all of the tasks, owners, and due dates related to implementing the course.**

This includes the time spent...

- Publishing the course into the Learning Management System (LMS).

- Communicating about the course.

- Measuring and reporting on the effectiveness of the course.

- Conducting a project retrospective.

# What Do You Think?

**What other implementation tasks might you want to list in your timeline?**

_____

_____

_____

_____

_____

**When creating your project timeline, remember the following...**

### Focus on Deliverables

When creating your eLearning project schedule, start by listing all the milestones and deliverables. How detailed you choose to get with your list of deliverables is up to you. I suggest focusing on the actual deliverable items rather than the high-level processes. For example, if you'll be delivering several drafts of a storyboard, list each draft as an item on your timeline. Because your SMEs also have items to deliver, such as storyboard edits, include them in your timeline, as well.

### Clearly Define Each Owner

Once you've created a comprehensive list of each deliverable item, identify who is responsible for each item. This is important, as it's very common for a subject matter expert to underestimate their required level of involvement. In addition to keeping your project on track, listing who is responsible for each deliverable creates accountability between you and your stakeholders and SMEs.

### Assign Realistic Delivery Dates

After you've listed all of the deliverable items and responsibilities, assign delivery dates for each item. As you do this, remember to be realistic about how much can get accomplished in any given block of time. Meetings, days off, other projects, and the availability of other people can easily affect your eLearning project schedule. Make sure your stakeholders and subject matter experts agree to their responsibilities listed on the timeline. If they're unable to meet a defined deadline, adjust the timeline accordingly.

## Which tools should I use to create my project plan & timeline?

You should use whichever tools work best for you. If you want to start with something simple, I'd suggest creating your project plan and timeline in Microsoft Word or something similar. If you like to use something more advanced, you can try Microsoft Project, which is specifically designed for creating and managing project timelines. You can also search for "project management software" online and find countless free and paid project management tools. Like I said, choose what works best for you!

## How long should it take me to build an eLearning course?

This is a common question that is regularly asked and debated within our industry. Usually, you see this question asked by corporate learning executives, desperately trying to timebox and budget for the amount of time it takes their teams to build a course and get on to the next one. And, yes, if you do some Googling, you'll find all sorts of interesting studies, research, and articles on the topic.

And you want to know what I think? I think most of it is B.S.! Here's the thing: how long it takes to develop an eLearning course (or any learning) depends on the unique variables you're currently facing.

- How complex is the content, and how much of it are you including?

- How much interactivity are you building into your course?

- Are you using stock graphics or custom graphics?

- Will there be audio narration, or will it be a text-based course?

- What tools are you using to develop the course, and what's your expertise with these tools?

- How many people need to review the course, how long will it take them to provide feedback, and how much feedback will they provide?

Each of these variables can have a significant impact on the time it takes you to develop a course. So, when creating your timeline, consider each of the variables and make your estimate according to what you think. Over time, you'll get a better sense of how much time you need to schedule for design and development.

# DESIGN A LEARNING SOLUTION

---

**In this chapter, you'll explore...**

- How to collect your training content.

- How to write learning objectives.

- How to design a blended training solution.

---

# NOTES

# DESIGN A LEARNING SOLUTION

**You need to know what you're going to build before you build it.**

Earlier in this book, I explained how the design and development of training, especially eLearning, is a lot like building a house. It starts by understanding the needs of the future homeowner, which is a lot like conducting a needs analysis to determine the training needs. From there, an architect drafts a blueprint, which allows the future homeowner to easily make changes before construction begins.

So, how does this apply when designing training, including eLearning? Well, if this were a book solely focused on eLearning, we'd just move straight into drafting a storyboard, which is a lot like a blueprint for a house. However, I'd be remiss if I didn't talk about the holistic approach to design—regardless of the training intervention that you're creating.

Whether you call yourself an eLearning designer, a trainer, a learning professional, or an instructional designer, it's your job to consider all of the possible ways you can create training experiences that promote the best learning outcomes. Yes, the solution might be an eLearning course; however, it could also be a simple job aid, an instructor-led workshop, or a mixture of them all.

## What Is Design?

When you're starting any new training project, especially large-scale training programs, it's easy to become overwhelmed trying to ideate and agree with your stakeholders on all of the various deliverables and how they fit together. This is especially true when you're targeting many different learners, with many different topics, and many different training modalities.

## You need to know what you're going to build before you start building it.

What you don't want to do is rush into development, without having a clear plan for how you're going to tackle it. After completing the design process, you'll have a clear plan of action for what you need to actually build during the development process.

---

**After completing the design process, you should be able to answer the following questions...**

What topics will be covered during the training?

Who are the learners who will recieve the training?

What will learners be able to do once the training is complete?

How will the training be delivered?

How will the training be measured?

---

## Aren't these questions answered during the needs analysis?

Sure! It's possible you might walk away from your needs analysis with many of these questions answered. However, remember: the purpose of a needs analysis isn't to determine how training might address the performance issue(s) you're examining, it's to determine the root cause of the performance issue and whether or not training might be a solution. If you determine that training is a solution, then it's very possible you'll have already determined the answers to many of these questions.

## What Do You Think?

**What other questions do you need to answer during the design process?**

_____

_____

_____

## Collect the Learning Content

When you're starting the design of your training solution, whether it's a blended solution or just a single eLearning course, the first step is to collect the raw content. This becomes the basis for determining which topics will be covered during the training. If you're new to instructional design and eLearning, one misconception that you may have is that your subject matter experts will provide you with all of the content you need to create your training. In fact, when I was early on in my eLearning career, I'd found myself wasting a ton of time, waiting for my subject matter experts to deliver everything they wanted me to include in the course.

## Don't expect your SMEs to magically come through with a deck that you can simply polish into a learner-ready eLearning course!

The truth is, while your subject matter experts may have some documented content, best practices, or procedures they can share with you, don't expect them to magically come through with a deck that you can simply polish into a learner-ready course! As eLearning (and instructional) designers, it's our job not only to collect content but also create it!

**Here are some ways you can collect your learning content...**

Talk to Your SMEs

Yes, I know I started this section by stating that you shouldn't rely on your SMEs for your learning content; however, it doesn't mean they can't be a trusted resource! As you organize and collect your learning content, spend some time interviewing your subject matter experts—they have a wealth of knowledge on the topic you're covering. While your SMEs will no doubt have a lot to say, be careful not to include everything they have to say. Oftentimes, they'll include a lot of nice-to-know information that your learners don't absolutely need.

**Review Best Practices**

As you collect your learning content, review any documented information and make sure your content aligns with the existing guidance and procedures. Oftentimes, you may discover that a discrepancy or gap exists between the information provided by your SMEs and what's documented in the best practices. If that's the case, bring this to the attention of your SMEs to be clarified and corrected.

**Conduct a Task Analysis**

If you're creating training on a task or procedure that has specific steps or procedures, a task analysis is a great way to systematically identify each task and process your learners need to perform. This can help ensure your learning objectives are aligned with what learners really need to be able to do after completing your course. Oftentimes, conducting a task analysis can help you better understand the topic of your training.

**Talk To & Observe Your Learners**

Observing and talking to those members of your audience who've already mastered the topic or process you're teaching is another great way to collect your training content. When you spend time talking to your learners, you get to understand what challenges they are facing and what they need to overcome those challenges. Of course, when you talk with those folks who've already mastered what you're teaching, you can draw from their experiences and build it into your training content.

# What Do You Think?

**When you're creating training, how do you go about collecting your content?**

_____

_____

_____

## How do I conduct a task analysis?

Great question! Here's my three-step process for conducting a task analysis...

**Identify the Primary Procedure**

The first step for conducting a task analysis is to identify the primary procedure your learners are expected to perform. When identifying the primary procedure, you want to avoid being too broad, which could result in performing a task analysis on something that should actually be separated out into multiple procedures. In this case, we'll look at the procedure of "completing the daily finance audit."

**List the Main Tasks**

The second step in conducting a task analysis is to identify and list the main tasks for completing the primary procedure. Similar to identifying the primary procedure, you don't want to be too broad or too specific. When listing the main tasks, and the subtasks, use action verbs to describe each task. For example, for our procedure of "completing the daily finance audit," it might look something like this:

1. Download the daily finance report.
2. Review the daily finance report for inaccuracies.
3. Report inaccuracies to the corporate finance auditor.

**List the Subtasks**

The third and final step for conducting an eLearning task analysis is to break the main tasks into subtasks. The subtasks are where you start getting granular with the level of details of each task. Using the first main task from our example of "completing the daily finance audit," here's what the final task analysis might look like, broken down into subtasks:

1. Download the daily finance report:
   a. Log in to the finance operating mainframe.
   b. Click the Run Daily Report button.
   c. Click the Download Daily Report button.

When you're starting work on a learning project, it's not always clear what information should and should not be included in your course. How can you separate nice-to-know information from must-know information, especially when it's a topic or process you aren't familiar with? While you might assume your subject matter experts will help you with this, don't hold your breath!

Here's the thing about subject matter experts: they want everyone to be just as passionate and informed as they are about their given area of expertise. Not only is this unrealistic, more often than not, it's also not really necessary. Your learners only need the minimal amount of information to do their jobs at the expected level of performance. That's it! There's nothing more and nothing less.

## Learners don't need to know things; they need to do things!

When working with your subject matter experts, ask questions that reveal the true relevancy of the content they are asking you to include. Instead of asking questions like, "Do we need to include this?" or "Is this information important?", ask questions like:

- How will employees use this information to complete the task?

- What would happen if employees didn't receive this information?

- Do employees need to memorize this information, or can it be referenced on-the-job?

# What Do You Think?

**What are some other ways you can identify and remove nice-to-know information?**

_____

_____

_____

# Define the Learning Objectives

Once you've collected and sorted through all of your training content, the next step in the design process is to define the learning objectives. Learning objectives play a critical role in the creation of any training content, as they define the outcomes or final results of the learning.

## Learning objectives define the outcomes or final results of the learning.

When written properly, learning objectives can be used to help define the scope of a training or an eLearning project and can act as an indicator for the amount of content that needs to be covered. They can also help you avoid scope creep, as learning objectives can help you remove or avoid content that doesn't support the final learning (i.e., nice-to-know information). Of course, learning objectives can act as a foundation in which to measure the effectiveness of your learning content, which we'll explore later in this book.

As you start to define your learning objectives, you'll likely struggle with how broad or specific you need to be. This is why it's important to understand the different types of learning objectives.

---

**Learning objectives usually fall into two categories...**

### Terminal Objectives

Terminal objectives define the overall learning or performance outcome(s). Typically, terminal objectives are used at the curriculum level, defining the overall performance outcome(s) for the entire training program.

### Enabling Objectives

Enabling objectives break down the terminal objective into smaller, more specific objectives. Typically, enabling objectives are used at the individual course level.

---

**How are learning objectives written?**

While it might seem simple to blurt out a couple of statements regarding what your learners will know or be able to do after the training is complete, the truth is, there's a science to writing them out correctly. Following a standard structure enables you to define learning objectives that are consistent and measurable.

**The anatomy of a learning objective contains three components...**

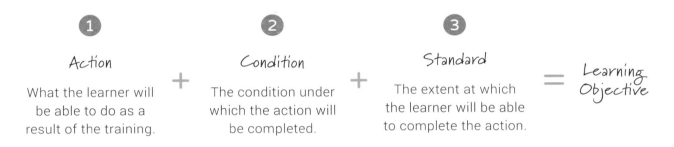

**1**

Action

What the learner will be able to do as a result of the training.

+

**2**

Condition

The condition under which the action will be completed.

+

**3**

Standard

The extent at which the learner will be able to complete the action.

=

Learning Objective

# What Do You Think?

**Do you write learning objectives when creating training content? If not, why?**
**What struggles do you encounter when attempting to define your learning objectives?**

_____

_____

_____

_____

**First, start by identifying the actions.**

Learning objectives typically begin with an action verb, used to describe the action to be completed or the behavior to be observed. The most common approach to writing learning objectives and defining the actions is by using Bloom's Taxonomy, which classified learning objectives into six levels of complexity and specificity.

When selecting an action verb, it often helps to consider what specific behavior you would actually observe in real life, which would validate the mastery of the task.

| Level | Description | Action Verbs |
|---|---|---|
| 1 Remembering | Recognizing and recalling facts. | List, Define, Tell, Describe, Identify, Show, Name, etc. |
| 2 Understanding | Understanding what the facts mean. | Explain, Describe, Discuss, Contrast, Predict, etc. |
| 3 Applying | Applying the facts, rules, concepts, or ideas. | Demonstrate, Complete, Illustrate, Show, Solve, etc. |
| 4 Analyzing | Breaking down information into component parts. | Analyze, Select, Distinguish, Order, Connect, Classify, etc. |
| 5 Evaluating | Judging the value of information or ideas. | Assess, Recommend, Decide, Rank, Grade, Test, etc. |
| 6 Creating | Combing parts to make a new whole. | Create, Integrate, Plan, Rewrite, Design, etc. |

Some verbs should be avoided, as they aren't specific or measurable. Examples include: appreciate, become, believe, grow, improve, know, learn, understand, etc.

### Then, determine the conditions.

After you've defined the action of your learning objective, the next step is to identify the condition. Conditions help to align your learning objectives in context with real-life circumstances. In other words, they describe the conditions under which the learner will perform the action.

### Finally, list the standards.

The final component of a learning objective is the standard. The standard defines the extent at which the learner will be able to complete the task. In other words, the standard describes the measurement of success.

Standards are often excluded from learning objectives, as they are quantitative, and many tasks, especially soft skills, are qualitative and hard to measure. Sometimes the desired quantitative measurement is a performance standard that can't be measured during the learning experience.

# What Do You Think?

**When you write learning objectives, do they usually contain conditions and standards? If so, can you provide some examples?**

_____

_____

_____

_____

## Do I need to share the learning objectives with my learners?

Gosh, I never thought you'd ask! Too often, courses start with these poorly designed screens that list each of the learning objectives. While it might seem nice to let your learners "in" on what you're going to cover, listing each of your learning objectives is not only ineffective and boring, it's also a total waste of time.

Instead, tell you learners how the course will provide value in their lives. This might mean opening your course with an animated story, explaining how they'll be able to sell more products or save more time. Whatever the case might be, learning objectives are simply there to help us design an effective and measurable course. That's it!

## Learning Objective Examples

(Action)   (Condition)   (Standard)

**Example One**

After completing this course, the learner will be able to complete a customer transaction using the point of sale system, while maintaining a customer satisfaction score of 80% or above.

**Example Two**

After completing this course, the learner will be able to submit an expense report using the travel expense system with no errors.

**Example Three**

After completing this course, the learner will be able to resolve a customer complaint using the online troubleshooting manual in less than 20 minutes.

**Example Four**

After completing this course, the learner will be able to complete the inventory certification exam without using notes and with a score of 90% or greater.

## Determine The Training Modalities

Any time you start work on a new learning project, someone will asks how you think the learning content should be delivered. Should it be an eLearning course or an instructor-led training? Should it be a how-to video or a job aid? The truth is, when I first started in the world of learning and development, I thought everything could be fixed with an eLearning course!

Creating an effective training program isn't a binary choice between one thing or another—eLearning vs. instructor-led training or video vs. a job aid.

Of course, now, it's easy for me to realize that how I viewed the creation of a training intervention was all wrong. As I mentioned earlier in this book, learning isn't a single event that occurs while seated in a classroom or behind the screen of an eLearning course. Learning is a process of experiences that occur over a period of time.

Because of this, I don't subscribe to the idea that training is a binary choice between one thing and another. It's not an eLearning vs. an instructor-led training, or a video vs. a job aid. Training should be a blend of experiences that promotes the long-term learning process.

Yes, while this book is focused primarily on the design and development of eLearning content, it's important to understand how you might create a blended learning solution, which may or may not incorporate eLearning.

**Do you know why you've chosen eLearning in the first place?**

Before I share with you my simple method for designing a blended learning solution, I think it's important for you to recognize and understand why you might have chosen eLearning in the first place. Yes, eLearning offers a ton of benefits; however, it's not always the learner that is on the receiving end of those benefits. Oftentimes, eLearning is chosen as the desired training modality, not for what it can offer your learners, but for what it can offer your organization.

For every fat eLearning course, there's a skinny job aid waiting to break free!

### Benefits for the Organization

- eLearning can track learner progress via a learning management system.

- eLearning can be created once and delivered to multiple learners.

- eLearning can offer a consistent message of content.

### Benefits for the Learner

- eLearning can be taken when and where it is convenient for the learner.

- eLearning can let learners practice skills in a safe, simulated environment.

- eLearning can be revisited and taken multiple times if necessary.

## What Do You Think?

**What are some of the reasons why you or your organization are interested in using eLearning as a training solution? How do they compare with the items you listed above?**

_____

_____

_____

**Design a blended training solution.**

Fortunately, designing a blended training solution is far easier than it might seem. It's simply a matter of identifying the learning outcomes you want to achieve and pairing them with one or more training objects. A great way to do this is by referencing your learning objectives. This can help you identify everything you need to achieve through the training and make an informed decision on which modalities to use.

Designing a blended training solution is simply a matter of identifying the learning outcomes and pairing them with one or more training objects.

For example, let's say you needed to create a training solution for a new piece of software your employees will need to use. Yes, you could create a single eLearning course and hope your learners will remember everything they need to know. On the other hand, you could try creating a blended solution, with multiple training modalities, used to support the learning process.

# What Do You Think?

**How could you go beyond just a single eLearning course and create a blended training solution for the example described above?**

_____

_____

_____

### How do you design a blended training solution?

When designing a blended training solution, you'll likely need to identify how you'll tackle most, if not all, of the possible learning outcomes. Ultimately, it depends on the topic of the training and what level of mastery you're looking to achieve with your learners.

In some cases, you may only need to transfer knowledge, which could be achieved with a single training object. In other situations, you may need to achieve multiple learning outcomes, which might require one or more training objects.

| Learning Outcomes | Training Objects | |
|---|---|---|
|  Transfer of Knowledge | ■ Lecture / Presentation<br>■ Explainer Video<br>■ Infographic<br>■ Job Aid<br>■ Article / Blog | ■ Communications<br>■ Podcast<br>■ Group Discussion<br>■ Observation<br>■ Etc. |
|  Practice of Task or Behaviors | ■ Roleplay<br>■ Digital Scenario<br>■ System Simulation | ■ Decision-Based Quiz<br>■ Trial & Error<br>■ Etc. |

| Learning Outcomes | Training Objects |
|---|---|

**Application of Tasks or Behaviors**

- System Simulation
- On-the-Job Practice
- Observation
- Coaching & Feedback
- Etc.

**Assessment of Knowledge or Performance**

- Knowledge-Based Quiz
- Decision-Based Quiz
- Performance Assessment
- Observation
- KPIs
- Etc.

**Just-in-Time Performance Support**

- Job Aid
- Online Resource
- Handouts
- Video Tutorial
- Article / Blog
- In-System Prompts
- Documented Best Practices
- Etc.

### How does blended training improve learning retention?

Earlier in the book, when we explored how people learn, I explained how learning isn't an event but rather a process. This means your learners won't master a skill just because they completed your eLearning course or attended your workshop.

For example, when training is delivered as a single event, initial learning retention is high. Once learners have completed the training event and return to their jobs and everyday lives, this is where the forgetting curve sets in. Your learners start to forget what they practiced during training, and before you know it, everything is lost.

## With blended learning, you can improve learning retention by offering opportunities for retraining and support.

On the other hand, with spaced and blended training events, you can fight against the forgetting curve by offering opportunities for retraining and support. This might come in the form of a job aid, a video, coaching, feedback, or any type of performance support that reengages the learner with the knowledge and skills initially taught during the main training event.

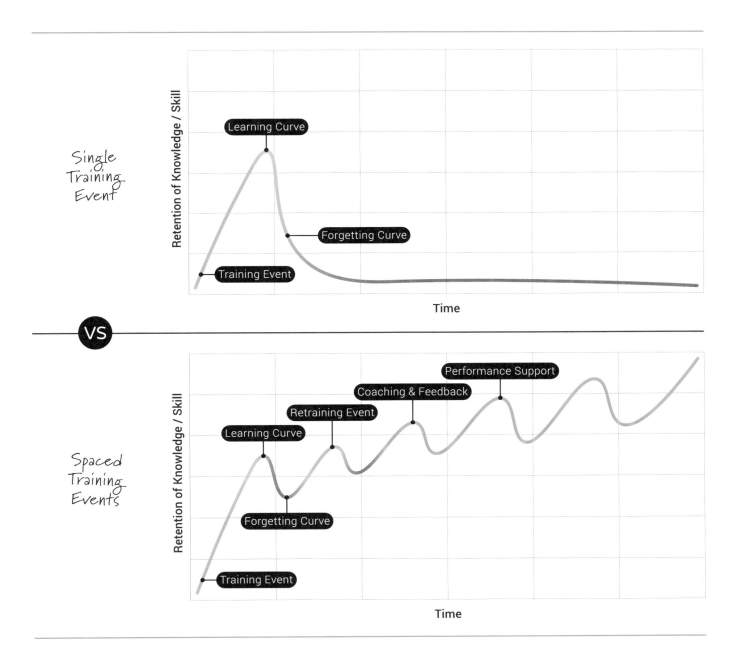

## Create a Design Document

Once you've collected your learning content (and removed nice-to-know information), defined the learning objectives, and determined the training modalities, the next step is to make sure your stakeholders and subject matter experts agree. What you don't want to do is move forward into development, without first making sure you're all on the same page. The best way to do this is to organize your plan into a design document.

A design document is used to provide a high-level overview of a training curriculum, comprised of several training objects or modalities.

## What's included in a design document?

While design documents come in many different shapes and sizes, it's my opinion that a design document should list...

- The topics that will be covered during the training.

- The target audience(s) for the training.

- The learning objectives that will be achieved after the training is complete.

- The learning objects that will be delivered during the training.

- How each topic / learning objective will be measured.

## DESIGN DOCUMENT

| TOPIC | AUDIENCE | LEARNING OBJECTIVES | MODALITY | MEASUREMENT |
|---|---|---|---|---|
| Introduction to the New Consultative Framework | All frontline sales employees and leaders | After receiving this email blast, sales employees and leaders will be able to:<br><br>• Describe the purpose of the new consultative sales framework and when it's launching. | Three-week email campaign | Email open and click rates |
| How to Greet the Customer | Frontline sales employees with more than 50% sales close rate | After completing this video and reading the associated job aid, sales employees will be able to:<br><br>• Construct a personalized greeting and use it when interacting with customers. | Explainer video and job aid | Customer satisfaction survey, question two re: greeting |
| How to Construct & Present a Solution | Frontline sales employees with more than 50% sales close rate | After completing this eLearning course, sales employees will be able to:<br><br>• Ask open-ended probing questions.<br>• Construct and present a solution to the customer.<br>• Overcome customer objections. | Self-Paced eLearning | Sales close rates and customer satisfaction survey results |
| How to Ask Probing Questions | Frontline sales employees with more than 50% sales close rate | After referencing this job aid, sales employees will be able to:<br><br>• Ask open-ended and informed questions when interacting with customers. | Job aid | Click rates |
| Overall Consultative Sales Framework | Frontline sales employees with less than 50% sales close rate | After attending this in-person workshop, sales employees will be able to:<br><br>• Demonstrate each of the five steps on the consulting framework when interacting with customers. | In-person workshop | Sales close rates and customer satisfaction survey results |
| How to Provide Coaching & Feedback for Leaders | All sales leaders | After attending this in-person workshop, sales leaders will be able to:<br><br>• Provide coaching and actionable guidance to their sales employees during 1:1 meetings. | In-person workshop | Sales close rates and customer satisfaction survey results |
| How to Measure Sales Effectiveness | All sales leaders | After referencing this job aid, sales leaders will be able to:<br><br>• Research and analyze sales data to offer effective coaching and guidance to sales employees. | Job aid | Click rates |

# TOPIC

**Introduction to the New Consultative Framework**

## DESIGN DOCUMENT

**How to Greet the Customer**

**How to Construct & Present a Solution**

**How to Ask Probing Questions**

**Overall Consultative Sales Framework**

**How to Provide Coaching & Feedback for Leaders**

**How to Measure Sales Effectiveness**

| AUDIENCE | LEARNING OBJECTIVES | MODALITY | MEASUREMENT |
|---|---|---|---|
| All frontline sales employees and leaders | After receiving this email blast, sales employees and leaders will be able to:<br><br>• Describe the purpose of the new consultative sales framework and when it's launching. | Three-week email campaign | Email open and click rates |
| Frontline sales employees with more than 50% sales close rate | After completing this video and reading the associated job aid, sales employees will be able to:<br><br>• Construct a personalized greeting and use it when interacting with customers. | Explainer video and job aid | Customer satisfaction survey, question two re: greeting |
| Frontline sales employees with more than 50% sales close rate | After completing this eLearning course, sales employees will be able to:<br><br>• Ask open-ended probing questions.<br>• Construct and present a solution to the customer.<br>• Overcome customer objections. | Self-Paced eLearning | Sales close rates and customer satisfaction survey results |
| Frontline sales employees with more than 50% sales close rate | After referencing this job aid, sales employees will be able to:<br><br>• Ask open-ended and informed questions when interacting with customers. | Job aid | Click rates |
| Frontline sales employees with less than 50% sales close rate | After attending this in-person workshop, sales employees will be able to:<br><br>• Demonstrate each of the five steps on the consulting framework when interacting with customers. | In-person workshop | Sales close rates and customer satisfaction survey results |
| All sales leaders | After attending this in-person workshop, sales leaders will be able to:<br><br>• Provide coaching and actionable guidance to their sales employees during 1:1 meetings. | In-person workshop | Sales close rates and customer satisfaction survey results |
| All sales leaders | After referencing this job aid, sales leaders will be able to:<br><br>• Research and analyze sales data to offer effective coaching and guidance to sales employees. | Job aid | Click rates |

All frontline sales
employees and leaders

GN DOCUMENT

Frontline sales employees
with more than 50% sales
close rate

Frontline sales employees
with more than 50% sales
close rate

Frontline sales employees
with more than 50% sales
close rate

Frontline sales employees
with less than 50% sales
close rate

All sales leaders

All sales leaders

| TOPIC | | ...ING OBJECTIVES | MODALITY | MEASUREMENT |
|---|---|---|---|---|
| Introduction to the N... Consultative Framew... | | ...g this email blast, sales employees and leaders ...: ...the purpose of the new consultative sales ...rk and when it's launching. | Three-week email campaign | Email open and click rates |
| How to Greet the Customer | | ...ing this video and reading the associated job ...loyees will be able to: ...t a personalized greeting and use it when ...g with customers. | Explainer video and job aid | Customer satisfaction survey, question two re... greeting |
| How to Construct & Present a Solution | | ...ing this eLearning course, sales employees will ...-ended probing questions. ...t and present a solution to the customer. ...e customer objections. | Self-Paced eLearning | Sales close rates and customer satisfaction survey results |
| How to Ask Probing Questions | | ...ing this job aid, sales employees will be able to: ...-ended and informed questions when ...g with customers. | Job aid | Click rates |
| Overall Consultative Sales Framework | | ...g this in-person workshop, sales employees will ...rate each of the five steps on the consulting ...rk when interacting with customers. | In-person workshop | Sales close rates and customer satisfaction survey results |
| How to Provide Coaching & Feedbac... for Leaders | | ...g this in-person workshop, sales leaders will be ...oaching and actionable guidance to their sales ...s during 1:1 meetings. | In-person workshop | Sales close rates and customer satisfaction survey results |
| How to Measure Sales Effectiveness | | ...ing this job aid, sales leaders will be able to: ...and analyze sales data to offer effective ...and guidance to sales employees. | Job aid | Click rates |

# LEARNING OBJECTIVES

After receiving this email blast, sales employees and leaders will be able to:

- Describe the purpose of the new consultative sales framework and when it's launching.

After completing this video and reading the associated job aid, sales employees will be able to:

- Construct a personalized greeting and use it when interacting with customers.

After completing this eLearning course, sales employees will be able to:

- Ask open-ended probing questions.
- Construct and present a solution to the customer.
- Overcome customer objections.

After referencing this job aid, sales employees will be able to:

- Ask open-ended and informed questions when interacting with customers.

After attending this in-person workshop, sales employees will be able to:

- Demonstrate each of the five steps on the consulting framework when interacting with customers.

After attending this in-person workshop, sales leaders will be able to:

- Provide coaching and actionable guidance to their sales employees during 1:1 meetings.

After referencing this job aid, sales leaders will be able to:

- Research and analyze sales data to offer effective coaching and guidance to sales employees.

| TOPIC | AUDIENCE | MEASUREMENT |
|---|---|---|
| Introduction to the New Consultative Framework | All frontline employees a | Email open and click rates |
| How to Greet the Customer | Frontline sal with more th close rate | Customer satisfaction survey, question two re greeting |
| How to Construct & Present a Solution | Frontline sal with more th close rate | Sales close rates and customer satisfaction survey results |
| How to Ask Probing Questions | Frontline sal with more th close rate | Click rates |
| Overall Consultative Sales Framework | Frontline sal with less tha close rate | Sales close rates and customer satisfaction survey results |
| How to Provide Coaching & Feedback for Leaders | All sales lea | Sales close rates and customer satisfaction survey results |
| How to Measure Sales Effectiveness | All sales lea | Click rates |

# DESIGN DOCUM[ENT]

| TOPIC | AUDIENCE | LEARNING OBJECTIVES | MODALITY | [MEASU]REMENT |
|---|---|---|---|---|
| Introduction to the New Consultative Framework | All frontline sales employees and leaders | After receiving this email blast, sales employees and lea[ders] will be able to:<br><br>• Describe the purpose of the new consultative sales framework and when it's launching. | Three-week email campaign | [...]nd click rates |
| How to Greet the Customer | Frontline sales employees with more than 50% sales close rate | After completing this video and reading the associated [job] aid, sales employees will be able to:<br><br>• Construct a personalized greeting and use it when interacting with customers. | Explainer video and job aid | [...]isfaction [...]ion two re[...] |
| How to Construct & Present a Solution | Frontline sales employees with more than 50% sales close rate | After completing this eLearning course, sales employee[s will] be able to:<br><br>• Ask open-ended probing questions.<br>• Construct and present a solution to the customer[.]<br>• Overcome customer objections. | Self-Paced eLearning | [...]ates and [...]isfaction [...]s |
| How to Ask Probing Questions | Frontline sales employees with more than 50% sales close rate | After referencing this job aid, sales employees will be ab[le to]:<br><br>• Ask open-ended and informed questions when interacting with customers. | Job aid | |
| Overall Consultative Sales Framework | Frontline sales employees with less than 50% sales close rate | After attending this in-person workshop, sales employee[s will] be able to:<br><br>• Demonstrate each of the five steps on the consulti[ve] framework when interacting with customers. | In-person workshop | [...]ates and [...]isfaction [...]s |
| How to Provide Coaching & Feedback for Leaders | All sales leaders | After attending this in-person workshop, sales leaders w[ill be] able to:<br><br>• Provide coaching and actionable guidance to their employees during 1:1 meetings. | In-person workshop | [...]ates and [...]isfaction [...]s |
| How to Measure Sales Effectiveness | All sales leaders | After referencing this job aid, sales leaders will be able t[o]:<br><br>• Research and analyze sales data to offer effective coaching and guidance to sales employees. | Job aid | |

## DESIGN DOCUMENT

| TOPIC | AUDIENCE | LEARNING OBJECTIVES | MODALITY | MEASUREMENT |
|---|---|---|---|---|
| | | | | Email open and click rates |
| Introduction to the New Consultative Framework | All frontline sales employees and leaders | After receiving this email blast, sales employees and leaders will be able to:<br><br>• Describe the purpose of the new consultative sales framework and when it's launching. | Three-week email campaign | |
| How to Greet the Customer | Frontline sales employees with more than 50% sales close rate | After completing this video and reading the associated job aid, sales employees will be able to:<br><br>• Construct a personalized greeting and use it when interacting with customers. | Explainer video and | Customer satisfaction survey, question two re: greeting |
| How to Construct & Present a Solution | Frontline sales employees with more than 50% sales close rate | After completing this eLearning course, sales employees will be able to:<br><br>• Ask open-ended probing questions.<br>• Construct and present a solution to the customer.<br>• Overcome customer objections. | Self-Paced eLearnir | Sales close rates and customer satisfaction survey results |
| How to Ask Probing Questions | Frontline sales employees with more than 50% sales close rate | After referencing this job aid, sales employees will be able to:<br><br>• Ask open-ended and informed questions when interacting with customers. | Job aid | Click rates |
| Overall Consultative Sales Framework | Frontline sales employees with less than 50% sales close rate | After attending this in-person workshop, sales employees will be able to:<br><br>• Demonstrate each of the five steps on the consulting framework when interacting with customers. | In-person workshop | Sales close rates and customer satisfaction survey results |
| How to Provide Coaching & Feedback for Leaders | All sales leaders | After attending this in-person workshop, sales leaders will be able to:<br><br>• Provide coaching and actionable guidance to their sales employees during 1:1 meetings. | In-person workshop | Sales close rates and customer satisfaction survey results |
| How to Measure Sales Effectiveness | All sales leaders | After referencing this job aid, sales leaders will be able to:<br><br>• Research and analyze sales data to offer effective coaching and guidance to sales employees. | Job aid | Click rates |

# DRAFT A STORYBOARD

---

**In this chapter, you'll explore...**

- How to create a course outline.

- The different types of eLearning storyboards.

- How to draft your eLearning storyboard.

---

# NOTES

# DRAFT A STORYBOARD

**A storyboard is like a blueprint for your eLearning course.**

Okay, so you've conducted a needs analysis, collected your content, created a design document, and now, you're ready to start developing your eLearning course! Sounds great, right?! Well, where do you even begin?

When you're tasked with creating an eLearning course, especially if it's your first one, knowing where to start can be a bit confusing. I remember when I needed to start building my first eLearning course. I sat in front of my computer, unsure of what to do next. Was I supposed to start by opening a Word doc and drafting my content? Or, was I supposed to open PowerPoint and start creating some slides? The truth is, I had no idea where to start.

If you're new to eLearning, you've likely encountered this same issue. In my case, with my first eLearning course, after sitting in front of my computer for several hours trying to figure out where to begin, I learned that I needed to start by drafting my learning content. I needed to take a content-first strategy—designing my course and slides around my content, not the other way around. This is done by drafting a storyboard.

## Start By Drafting A Storyboard

Throughout this book, I've compared the design and development of an eLearning course to the design and construction of a house. When building a house, before an architect drafts a blueprint, they need to spend time with their client to determine their needs. How many bedrooms and bathrooms do they need? Do they need a two- or three-car garage? Would they like a modern design or something more traditional?

## A storyboard is like a blueprint for your eLearning course.

Once the architect has a strong understanding of their client's needs, they then draft a blueprint to show the client what their new house will look like and how it will be laid out. But what purpose does it serve the client to see the blueprints before construction begins? Why don't architects save time and simply jump to building the house after they've determined their client's needs?

Well, the answer is quite simple: the client might want to make changes before the house is built! What if the client wants to move the kitchen or add an extra bedroom? It's not exactly easy to make significant changes after the foundation has been poured and walls have been built. However, anything can be changed when it's just a simple drawing on paper. The same idea applies when designing an eLearning course.

### COMMON QUESTION

*Why should I start with a storyboard rather than jumping straight to development?*

When you're working with a group of stakeholders and SMEs, they will (or should) want to be involved in the development of the course. Since these folks likely don't understand how big of an impact a single edit can have on the course as a whole, you don't want to jump straight to development too early. For example, a small edit to how a fully-developed branching scenario works might result in hours of work for you to implement it into the design. However, when that branching scenario is just on paper, in a storyboard, making a change is just a matter of moving or rewriting some text. It's because of this that I recommend finalizing as much of the content in the storyboard stage before you move into full development.

### What is an eLearning storyboard?

An eLearning storyboard is simply a written document that outlines the learning content, slide-by-slide or screen-by-screen. The purpose of a storyboard is to provide your stakeholders and subject matter experts a preview of how the course will flow and how the content will be presented. The storyboard also gives reviewers the opportunity to easily make edits and change the course content before you begin development.

### Starting with an eLearning storyboard can help you...

Focus on
Your Content

Collaborate with Your
Stakeholders & SMEs

Quickly Incorporate
Feedback & Edits

# What Do You Think?

**Do you start your eLearning development process by drafting an eLearning storyboard? If so, how does it help your workflow?**

_____

_____

_____

_____

## Create A Course Outline

Getting started with writing the first draft of your storyboard is always a challenge. It's easy to feel overwhelmed and unsure about where to begin, especially as the raw content is piled upon your desk. So, what do you do?

Well, before you begin drafting your storyboard, I recommend starting with an outline. Creating an outline of your eLearning content can help you visualize how your content will be structured and how it will flow from one topic to another. This is also a great time to identify what content you might want to make interactive or what content you want to present visually on the screen. Finally, before you begin writing the first draft of your storyboard, sharing a high-level outline of your course with your stakeholders and subject matter experts can help you ensure you're on the right path.

### COMMON QUESTION

*How do I create an outline of my eLearning course?*

When creating an outline of your eLearning course, I recommend keeping it simple and easy to edit. For me, this involves sticky notes, a marker, and a wall.

**1** *List Each Topic*

Start by creating a sticky note for each of the main topics and subtopics that you'll be covering during the course.

**2** *Identify Interactivity*

If you plan to incorporate interactivity into your course, create a sticky note to indicate it. This includes knowledge checks, scenarios, and click-to-reveal interactions.

**3** *Organize the Flow*

Finally, organize your sticky notes to show how each topic and interaction will flow. If necessary, add a sticky note to indicate a main menu and draw arrows to show the flow of branching.

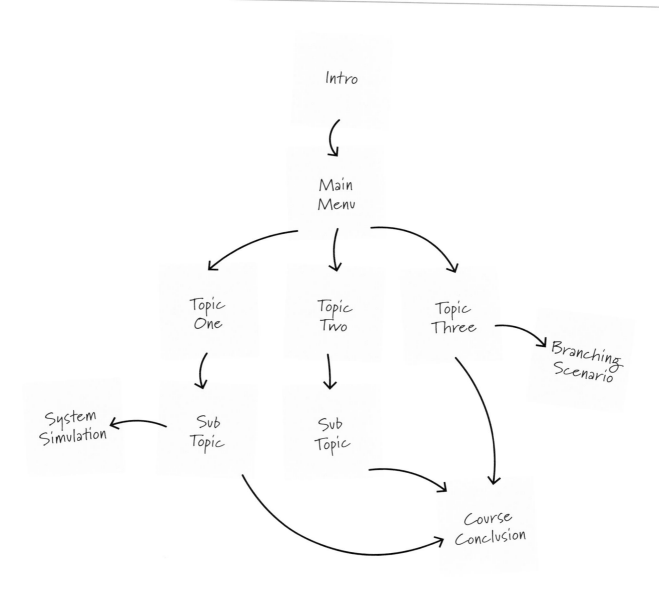

Intro

Main
Menu

Topic
One

Topic
Two

Topic
Three

Branching
Scenario

System
Simulation

Sub
Topic

Sub
Topic

Course
Conclusion

## Select a Storyboard Format

Before you can begin drafting your storyboard, you first need to select the format you'd like to use. An eLearning storyboard can come in many different formats, each with their own advantages and disadvantages.

Which storyboard format you choose to use for the development of your eLearning course depends on what you need to get out of it.

At the end of the day, it's important to remember that a storyboard is a tool, not just to help you plan and develop your course, but also to help you review it with your stakeholders and subject matter experts. The goal in creating a storyboard, like a blueprint for a house, is to make sure everyone involved understands and agrees to what you're going to build before you build it.

Typically, eLearning storyboards come in one of two formats: a written storyboard or a visual storyboard. Which one you choose ultimately depends on what you need to get out of it.

**Most eLearning storyboards come in one of two formats...**

## Written Storyboard

A written storyboard outlines your eLearning content slide-by-slide or screen-by-screen. Typically, a written storyboard includes a series of tables, which outlines the audio narration for each slide, as well as the on-screen graphics, text and technical functionality.

## Visual Storyboard

Like a written storyboard, a visual storyboard outlines your eLearning content slide-by-slide or screen-by-screen. However, a visual storyboard also includes simple mockups, using simple shapes and placeholders, which gives a rough idea of how each slide will be laid out.

# What Do You Think?

**Which storyboard format do you prefer to use and why?**

_____

_____

_____

## When does it make sense to use a written storyboard?

A written storyboard is ideal when you need to focus solely on the content and flow of your course. Additionally, written storyboards are easy to edit and iterate with your subject matter experts. For example, a small edit to how a fully developed branching scenario works might result in hours of work for you to implement it into the design. However, when that branching scenario is just on paper, in a storyboard, making a change is just a matter of moving or rewriting some text.

# WRITTEN STORYBOARD

## SLIDE 01 - INTRODUCTION

| Audio Narration | On-Screen Graphic & Text |
| --- | --- |
| Welcome to this course on our new consultative sales framework. During this course, we'll explore how you can consult with customers and offer tailored solutions to fit their needs.<br><br>Click the Begin button to get started. | **Text:**<br>Consultative Sales 101<br><br>**Graphics:**<br>One male and one female character<br><br>**Button:**<br>Begin |

**Technical Notes**

Learner clicks the Begin button to advance to course menu.

## SLIDE 02 - MAIN MENU

| Audio Narration | On-Screen Graphic & Text |
| --- | --- |
| Throughout this course, you'll get the chance to explore each of the five steps in our new consultative sales framework. You'll also put your skills into practice with real-life situations and scenarios.<br><br>To start learning how you can take your consultative sales skills to the next level, select a topic from the menu below. | **Text:**<br>Learn more about our new consultative sales framework by selecting a topic from the menu below.<br><br>**Buttons:**<br>Our Customers<br>Consultation Basics<br>Building Rapport<br>Offering a Solution<br>Closing the Sale |

**Technical Notes**

Learner clicks a menu item to be jumped to that section of the course. As the learner completes each section, they are returned to the main menu, where each menu item is checked off. Once the learner has viewed all items, they can proceed to the final section.

## SLIDE 03 - OUR CUSTOMERS

| Audio Narration | On-Screen Graphic & Text |
| --- | --- |
| We provide many different products and services to many different types of customers. The truth is, not all customers are the same. As a result, it's up to you to tailor your approach to each of the different customer types.<br><br>Click each customer to learn more. | **Text:**<br>We provide products and services to many different customers with many different needs. Click each customer to learn more.<br><br>**Graphics:**<br>Three different characters, representing our different types of customers. |

**Technical Notes**

Learner clicks on each customer, revealing a pop-up window, displaying additional information.

# WRITTEN STORYBOARD

## SLIDE 01 - INTRODUCTION

**Audio Narration**

Welcome to this course on our new consultative sales framework. During this course, we'll explore how you can consult with customers and offer tailored solutions to fit their needs.

Click the Begin button to get started.

**On-Screen Graphic & Text**

**Text:**
Consultative Sales 101

**Graphics:**
One male and one female character

**Button:**
Begin

**Technical Notes**

Learner clicks the Begin button to advance to course menu.

topic from the menu below

Our Customers
Consultation Basics
Building Rapport
Offering a Solution
Closing the Sale

Technical Notes

Learner clicks a menu item to be jumped to that section of the course. As the learner completes each section, they are returned to the main menu, where each menu item is checked off. Once the learner has viewed all items, they can proceed to the final section.

### SLIDE 03 - OUR CUSTOMERS

Audio Narration

We provide many different products and services to many different types of customers. The truth is, not all customers are the same. As a result, it's up to you to tailor your approach to each of the different customer types.

Click each customer to learn more.

On-Screen Graphic & Text

Text:
We provide products and services to many different customers with many different needs. Click each customer to learn more.

Graphics:
Three different characters, representing our different types of customers

Technical Notes

Learner clicks on each customer, revealing a pop-up window, displaying additional information.

# WRITTEN STORYBOARD

## SLIDE 01 - INTRODUCTION

**Audio Narration**

Welcome to this course on our new consultative sales framework. During this course, we'll explore how you can consult with customers and offer tailored solutions to fit their needs.

Click the Begin button to get started.

On-Screen Graphic & Text

**Text:**
Consultative Sales 101

**Graphics:**
One male and one female character.

**Button:**

## SLIDE 02 - MAIN MENU

**Audio Narration**

Throughout this course, you'll get the chance to explore each of the five steps in our new consultative sales framework. You'll also put your skills into practice with real-life situations and scenarios.

To start learning how you can take your consultative sales skills to the next level, select a topic from the menu below.

**On-Screen Graphic & Text**

**Text:**
Learn more about our new consultative sales framework by selecting a topic from the menu below.

**Buttons:**
Our Customers
Consultation Basics
Building Rapport
Offering a Solution
Closing the Sale

**Technical Notes**

Learner clicks a menu item to be jumped to that section of the course. As the learner completes each section, they are returned to the main menu, where each menu item is checked off. Once the learner has viewed all items, they can proceed to the final section.

We provide many different products and services to many different types of customers. The truth is, not all customers are the same. As a result, it's up to you to tailor your approach to each of the different customer types.

Click each customer to learn more.

Text:
We provide products and services to many different customers with many different needs. Click each customer to learn more.

Graphics:
Three different characters, representing our different types of customers.

Technical Notes

Learner clicks on each customer, revealing a pop-up window, displaying additional information.

# WRITTEN STORYBOARD

SLIDE 01 - INTRODUCTION

| Audio Narration | On-Screen Graphic & Text |
| --- | --- |
| Welcome to this course on our new consultative sales framework. During this course, we'll explore how you can consult with customers and offer tailored solutions to fit their needs. | Text: Consultative Sales 101 |
| Click the Begin button to get started. | Graphics: One male and one female character |
| | Button: Begin |

Technical Notes

Learner clicks the Begin button to advance to course menu.

SLIDE 02 - MAIN MENU

| Audio Narration | On-Screen Graphic & Text |
| --- | --- |
| Throughout this course, you'll get the chance to explore each of the five steps in our new consultative sales framework. You'll also put your skills into practice with real-life situations and scenarios. | Text: Learn more about our new consultative sales framework by selecting a topic from the menu below. |
| To start learning how you can take your consultative sales skills to the next level, select a topic from the menu below. | Buttons: Our Customers Consultation Basics Building Rapport |

## SLIDE 03 - OUR CUSTOMERS

| Audio Narration | On-Screen Graphic & Text |
| --- | --- |
| We provide many different products and services to many different types of customers. The truth is, not all customers are the same. As a result, it's up to you to tailor your approach to each of the different customer types. | **Text:** We provide products and services to many different customers with many different needs. Click each customer to learn more. |
| Click each customer to learn more. | **Graphics:** Three different characters, representing our different types of customers. |

**Technical Notes**

Learner clicks on each customer, revealing a pop-up window, displaying additional information.

## When does it make sense to use a visual storyboard?

A visual storyboard is ideal when you're working with reviewers who are familiar with the development process and can interpret the visual mockups. Some reviewers can become easily distracted from the content, providing feedback on items that aren't relevant during that point of the development cycle. For example, when you tell your reviewers to focus on the content, they inevitably get sidetracked, questioning your use of colors, placeholder images, etc.

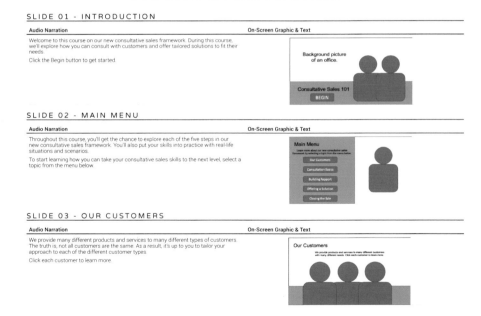

# VISUAL STORYBOARD

## SLIDE 01 - INTRODUCTION

**Audio Narration**

**On-Screen Graphic & Text**

Welcome to this course on our new consultative sales framework. During this course, we'll explore how you can consult with customers and offer tailored solutions to fit their needs.

Click the Begin button to get started.

Background picture of an office.

Consultative Sales 101

BEGIN

To start learning how you can take your consultative sales skills to the next level, select a topic from the menu below.

Our Customers

Consultation Basics

Building Rapport

Offering a Solution

Closing the Sale

## SLIDE 03 - OUR CUSTOMERS

**Audio Narration**

**On-Screen Graphic & Text**

We provide many different products and services to many different types of customers. The truth is, not all customers are the same. As a result, it's up to you to tailor your approach to each of the different customer types.

Click each customer to learn more.

Our Customers

We provide products and services to many different customers with many different needs. Click each customer to learn more.

# VISUAL STORYBOARD

## SLIDE 01 - INTRODUCTION

**Audio Narration**

Welcome to this course on our new consultative sales framework. During this course, we'll explore how you can consult with customers and offer tailored solutions to fit their needs.

Click the Begin button to get started.

**On-Screen Graphic & Text**

## SLIDE 02 - MAIN MENU

**Audio Narration**

Throughout this course, you'll get the chance to explore each of the five steps in our new consultative sales framework. You'll also put your skills into practice with real-life situations and scenarios.

To start learning how you can take your consultative sales skills to the next level, select a topic from the menu below.

**On-Screen Graphic & Text**

The truth is, not all customers are the same. As a result, it's up to you to tailor your approach to each of the different customer types.

Click each customer to learn more.

# VISUAL STORYBOARD

## SLIDE 01 - INTRODUCTION

**Audio Narration**

On-Screen Graphic & Text

Welcome to this course on our new consultative sales framework. During this course, we'll explore how you can consult with customers and offer tailored solutions to fit their needs.

Click the Begin button to get started.

## SLIDE 02 - MAIN MENU

**Audio Narration**

On-Screen Graphic & Text

Throughout this course, you'll get the chance to explore each of the five steps in our new consultative sales framework. You'll also put your skills into practice with real-life situations and scenarios.

# SLIDE 03 - OUR CUSTOMERS

**Audio Narration**

On-Screen Graphic & Text

We provide many different products and services to many different types of customers. The truth is, not all customers are the same. As a result, it's up to you to tailor your approach to each of the different customer types.

Click each customer to learn more.

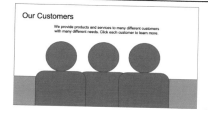

# Write the First Draft of Your Storyboard

Once you've determined what format you'll use to draft your eLearning storyboard, it's finally time to start writing it!

The truth is, writing the first draft of your storyboard is perhaps the most time-intensive and stressful part of the eLearning development process. It's where you finally "put pen to paper" and complete the arduous task of transforming all the raw content you've received into a development-ready storyboard.

Writing the first draft of your storyboard is perhaps the most time-intensive and stressful part of the eLearning development process.

If you've done a good job with your outline, the task of writing your first draft is simply a matter of filling in the gaps. At this point, you shouldn't need to worry about how the course will flow or what content will be covered. However, how you storyboard your course, what types of slides you include, and how you choose to make it interactive ultimately depends on the topic of your course and what you're looking to achieve with it.

Later in this book, we'll explore how you can increase learning retention and reduce cognitive load through the use of interactivity, visual design, and user interface design.

## COMMON QUESTION

### What tools should I use to draft my storyboard?

Fantastic question! The good news is: it's totally up to you! Personally, when I'm drafting a written storyboard, I like to use Microsoft Word or Google Docs. If I'm creating a visual storyboard, I'll usually stick with Microsoft PowerPoint.

Regardless of which tool you choose to use, each of these tools makes it easy to share your storyboards with your stakeholders and subject matter experts for review and feedback.

**How do you storyboard the different types of slides included in an eLearning course?**

As we explored at the beginning of this book, eLearning can come in many different formats. As a result, the types of slides you might include are nearly endless. This is especially true when you consider all of the different types of authoring tools and programs (which we'll look at later in this book) that you can use to create eLearning. How you storyboard each slide type depends on which on-screen actions will take place in the fully developed course.

**Most asynchronous (self-paced) eLearning includes four main types of slides...**

### Text-Based Slides

A text-based slide is a static, non-interactive slide, where the learning content is presented with only on-screen text, images, and graphics.

### Presentation Slides

A presentation slide is an animated, non-interactive slide, where the learning content is presented with animated text, images, and graphics usually synced with audio narration.

### Click-To-Reveal Slides

A click-to-reveal slide is an interactive slide, where the learning content is presented upon the learner clicking a button or some other interactive object.

### Decision-Based Slides

A decision-based slide is an interactive slide, where the learner is required to make some sort of knowledge- or skills-based decision.

### When storyboarding text-based slides...

- Consider how much text can be easily fit onto a single slide. Don't be afraid to break your content into multiple slides.
- Ensure your text content matches the reading level of your audience.
- Include detailed descriptions of any images or graphics that will accompany the on-screen text.

### When storyboarding presentation slides...

- Make sure your audio narration is written in a natural and conversational tone.
- Only script audio narration for content that you'll be able to visually communicate on the screen.
- Include detailed descriptions of what text, images, or graphics will animate in and out with your audio narration.

### When storyboarding click-to-reveal slides...

- Clearly indicate what items will be interactive or clickable.
- Describe what will happen when the learner clicks on each item (i.e., a pop-up window is revealed, etc.).
- Outline the content (text, images, graphics, videos, etc.) that will be revealed when the learner clicks on each interactive object.

### When storyboarding decision-based slides...

- Include details, describing what type of decision-based interaction is being storyboarded (i.e., quiz slide, branching scenario, etc.).
- Outline each of the options the learner can choose from and indicate what happens when they select each (i.e., jumps to another slide, presents feedback, etc.).
- Describe any feedback that will be presented to the learner when they select a correct / incorrect option.

# What Do You Think?

What other tips do you have for storyboarding text-based slides?

_____

_____

_____

What other tips do you have for storyboarding presentation slides?

_____

_____

_____

What other tips do you have for storyboarding click-to-reveal slides?

_____

_____

_____

What other tips do you have for storyboarding decision-based slides?

_____

_____

_____

## How long should I make my eLearning course?

I'm glad you asked! I remember a time when the general rule was that an eLearning course should be no more than one hour long! This eventually turned into 30 minutes, then 15 minutes, and now, it hovers between 5 and 10 minutes.

The problem with this question is that it assumes there's an ideal length for how long learning takes. The truth is: learning takes as long as it needs to take. As much as it would be convenient to make a one-size-fits-all guideline for eLearning, it always depends on the complexity of the content, the level of mastery you're looking to achieve through the learning experience, and how much time your learners can dedicate to the training experience you create.

With that said, instead of asking how long an eLearning course should or shouldn't be, I would challenge you to ask yourself the following questions when designing your next eLearning course...

- What level of effort will it take for learners to reach the desired level of performance?
- How much time can learners dedicate to formal training in a single sitting?
- How can we chunk and structure the information to be as effective as possible?

How you answer these questions will help you create the most effective eLearning course, tailored to the needs of your learners, the organization, and your goals.

## What Do You Think?

**Do you think there's an "ideal" length for an eLearning course? If so, what is it and why?**

_____

_____

_____

## Review & Edit Your Storyboard

So, you've finished the first draft of your eLearning storyboard, and now it's time to hand it over to your stakeholders and subject matter experts for review. This will be the first time they get to see the fruits of your labor, and you want to ensure they have ample opportunity to provide feedback.

The review process, at every stage of the eLearning development process, is crucial for the successful delivery of the course. It's especially important during storyboard development, as it's during this stage when it's easiest to make changes. However, don't expect to simply hand over the storyboard to reviewers who know exactly what kind of feedback to provide.

## The onus is on us to make the review process as simple as possible!

In my experience, I've found that most stakeholders and subject matter experts underestimate their level of involvement in the development of an eLearning course. They often assume their job is to provide the content on the front end and then approve the final course on the back end. They don't realize they have to review the course at each stage of development. The truth is: the onus is on us, as eLearning developers, to make the review process as simple as possible—especially if we want that feedback on time!

**Provide clear instructions on what needs to be reviewed and by when.**

Before letting your stakeholders and subject matter experts run off to review your storyboard, you want to provide very clear instructions on what you need them to review and by when. For example, you don't want your reviewers getting caught up in the number of slides you're building into the course, especially when you need them to ensure the accuracy of the learning content.

**Schedule review time on your SME's calendar.**

We all know that stakeholders and subject matter experts are busy folks. In addition to the time you're asking them to dedicate to the development and review of your eLearning course, SMEs also have full-time jobs to attend to!

Make it easier to get feedback on your storyboard by sending a calendar invite (with a link to the storyboard) for dedicated review time. This invite isn't meant for you to meet with them to review your storyboard but rather to help your SMEs dedicate a block of time to reviewing it on their own.

**Conduct a Live Review Session**

One of the most efficient ways to manage your review cycles is to do it in-person. This lets you hear directly from the mouths of your SMEs to fully understand their feedback, ask questions, and make quick decisions regarding the edits provided.

Before you meet in-person, send your SMEs a link to review your storyboard, followed by an invite to meet, and discuss their feedback a few days later. This will force your SMEs to review the storyboard in preparation for the live review meeting.

---

### PRO TIP

When you meet with your stakeholders and subject matter experts to prepare them for reviewing your storyboard, it can help to remind them of the eLearning development process and why it's necessary to review a storyboard first. It's very common for at least one stakeholder to ask why you don't have a fully functional course ready for them to review.

---

## What if my reviewers don't provide feedback on time or at all?

With some reviewers, you'll need to be a bit more forceful to get the feedback you need. You'll learn quickly which stakeholders are dependable and which ones need a bit more "help." If you have reviewers who regularly fail to provide feedback on time, I'd suggest scheduling a meeting and forcing them into a room. They will either arrive with their feedback or you can use the time to conduct a live feedback session.

## What if my reviewers provide conflicting feedback?

It's very common for reviewers to provide conflicting feedback. In these situations, I like to put the final decision in *their* hands. Again, I'll usually schedule a quick meeting, give them context about the conflicting feedback, and then let them decide who is right.

# What Do You Think?

**What other strategies can you use to get timely feedback from your stakeholders and SMEs?**

_____

_____

_____

_____

# DEVELOP THE COURSE

---

**In this chapter, you'll explore...**

- ■ How to select an eLearning authoring tool.

- ■ The different types of eLearning prototypes.

- ■ How to develop a prototype of your course.

---

# NOTES

_____

_____

_____

_____

_____

_____

_____

_____

_____

_____

_____

_____

_____

_____

_____

_____

_____

_____

# DEVELOP THE COURSE

**It's finally time to start building the darn thing!**

A lot of work has led you to this point. You've met with your stakeholders, asked them a boatload of questions, created a project plan and timeline, outlined a learning solution, and drafted a storyboard. Now, it's finally time to start building your eLearning course!

Did you ever think you'd do so much work before you actually arrived at this point?! The truth is: all the work you do *before* you start building your eLearning course is what ultimately determines its success. That's because, with training, it's garbage in, garbage out. You can build the most beautiful course in the world, but if you didn't plan it properly and ensure it's actually addressing performance issues, it's all a waste of time.

Fortunately, if you've done a good job planning your course, the development process shouldn't be too much of a challenge. Just like building a house, if everyone has thoroughly reviewed and agreed to what is in the blueprint, there shouldn't be too many surprises during construction.

## Select An eLearning Authoring Tool

As I've mentioned several times throughout this book, developing an eLearning course is a lot like building a house. In the last chapter, we explored how your eLearning storyboard is a lot like a blueprint for a house. In this chapter, we'll continue comparing the concept of eLearning design to house construction, but this time we'll explore the actual tools and techniques used in building your eLearning course.

Building a house requires tools, materials, and solid craftsmanship. The same applies when developing an eLearning course: you need a tool to build the course, graphics and media to build your slides, and good design skills.

The first step in the development process is knowing what authoring tool(s) you're going to use to build your eLearning course.

### What is an eLearning authoring tool?

An eLearning authoring tool is a specialized software program specifically designed for creating interactive digital learning content. In the last several years, an explosion of new tools have hit the market, offering eLearning designers and organizations the ability to pick the tools that work best for them and their training content.

## Not all eLearning authoring tools are created equally.

As I write this, I realize you may not have a choice in the eLearning authoring tool you use to develop your eLearning course. If you work for a company, it's very likely that they've already invested in a specific tool for eLearning development. Regardless, it's good to know the variety of eLearning authoring tools available on the market, as you may one day have the opportunity to pick a tool for yourself or your organization.

However, it's important to know that not all eLearning authoring tools are created equally. As you think about which tool you'd like to use, there are several variables and considerations you need to take into account when selecting the right tool.

**When selecting an eLearning authoring tool, ask yourself...**

*What type of learning experience is the tool capable of creating?*

Not all eLearning authoring tools are equally capable. Some specialize in the creation of mobile-responsive learning, with limited interactivity, and others allow for custom interactivity. Pick the tool that best aligns with the learning experience you're trying to create.

*How much time do I have to develop the course?*

Depending on the tool you're using and the complexity of the content, some eLearning authoring tools require more development time than others. Pick the tool that best aligns with how much time you have to develop your course.

*How comfortable am I using this tool?*

Each eLearning authoring tool has its own unique learning curve. Some tools require zero programming knowledge, and others can be quite advanced. Pick the tool that best aligns with your current skill set.

# What Do You Think?

**What other considerations might affect which eLearning authoring tool you would use?**

_____

_____

_____

_____

_____

**Most eLearning authoring tools fall into the following categories...**

### Desktop-Based Tools

These tools are stand-alone programs, offering the ability to create highly interactive and custom eLearning content.

- Articulate Storyline
- Adobe Captivate
- Lectora

### Cloud-Based Tools

These tools are web-based and usually specialize in the creation of device-responsive eLearning content.

- Rise
- Lectora Online
- Gomo Learning

### PowerPoint-Based Tools

These tools exist as a PowerPoint add-on, letting you convert and publish PowerPoint slides into interactive eLearning content.

- Articulate Studio
- Adobe Presenter
- iSpring

### LMS-Based Tools

These tools are usually included within a learning management system, letting you combine text, images, video, and quizzes into an eLearning course.

- Most LMS Platforms

*This is not an all-inclusive list or an endorsement for any specific eLearning authoring tool. The tools listed above are current at the time of this writing.*

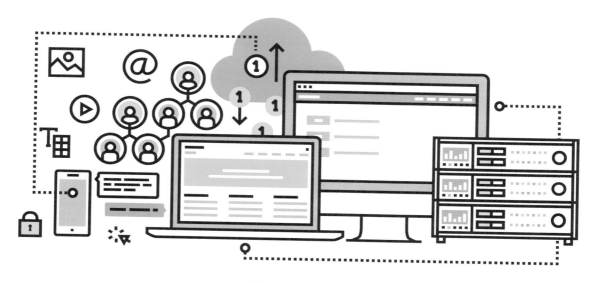

If you're not sure which eLearning authoring tool is right for you and your project, download and play with a free trial of a few different programs. Most, if not all, of the major eLearning authoring tool companies (including Articulate and Captivate) offer fully functional trials of their software.

# What Do You Think?

**Which eLearning authoring tool(s) are you familiar with? What do you like / dislike about each one?**

_____

_____

_____

_____

_____

## What other tools might I use in the development of my eLearning course?

In addition to your primary eLearning authoring tool, you may find that you need to use some additional tools in the creation of your eLearning course. Here are some of the tools I use on a regular basis...

### Graphic Design Tools

- Adobe Illustrator
- PowerPoint
- Canva

### Screen Recording Tools

- Camtasia
- Snagit
- Replay

### Video Editing Tools

- Camtasia
- Replay
- iMovie
- Windows Movie Maker
- Adobe Premiere Pro

### Audio Recording Tools

- Camtasia
- Audacity
- GarageBand
- Adobe Audition

### Photo Editing Tools

- Adobe Photoshop
- PowerPoint
- Snagit

## What Do You Think?

**What other tools would you add to the list?**

_____

_____

_____

# Develop a Prototype

After you've chosen the eLearning authoring tool you'd like to use to develop your eLearning course, the next step is to build a prototype of your course. If you think along the lines of building a house, a prototype is like a 3D model of the house that's about to be constructed. The 3D model gives the prospective homeowners an additional preview of the house after the blueprint has been drafted.

At this stage, the homeowners might realize they need to make the master bedroom a bit larger, add more windows, or even move the kitchen—things that can't be easily changed once construction begins.

## What is an eLearning prototype?

An eLearning prototype is simply a sample of your course. Just like a 3D model of a house, a prototype gives your stakeholders a preview of what the course will look like, how it will present the learning content, and how the interactivity will work. It's yet another opportunity for your stakeholders to make changes before you spend hours developing the entire course.

---

## Starting with an eLearning prototype can help you...

### Align Expectations

Because an eLearning prototype usually only contains a few slides, you can quickly get reactions from your stakeholders and subject matter experts *before* you invest the time in developing the entire course.

### Validate Functionality

Creating an eLearning prototype lets you ensure you can actually build the interactions you designed in your storyboard. Using placeholder text, images, and other graphics, you can quickly validate the technical functionality of your course.

## Select a Prototype Format

In the last chapter, I explained how an eLearning storyboard is a tool to help you plan and develop your course, and which format you use depends on what you need to get out of it. The same rules apply when selecting which format to use for your prototype.

The goal of creating a prototype is simple: to validate the design and functionality of your eLearning course before you develop the entire thing.

Sometimes, the prototype you develop is just for you to validate the functionality of your course, and other times, it's to validate the overall learning experience with your stakeholders and subject matter experts. Sometimes, you'll only create one prototype, and other times, you may end up creating multiple prototypes.

In either case, the goal of creating a prototype is to help you get through development without any surprises. What you don't want to do is develop your entire course, only to discover your stakeholders and subject matter experts want to change everything. This is not to say a prototype will prevent this outcome in every situation, but it will dramatically reduce the chances of it occurring.

**Most eLearning prototypes come in one of three formats...**

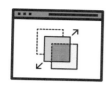

Wireframe Prototype

A wireframe prototype is used to validate the functionality of your eLearning course. Typically, a wireframe prototype uses simple placeholder text, images, and graphics—as the focus is more on the technical functionally of your course.

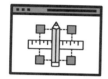

Visual Prototype

A visual prototype is used to validate the look and feel of your eLearning course. Although a visual prototype may or may not include actual content, the focus is more on the fonts, colors, images, graphics, animations, and overall layout of your slides.

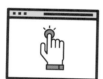

Functional Prototype

A functional prototype is a fully developed sample of your course, used to validate the overall learning experience. A functional prototype typically includes a small sampling of slides from the whole course—using actual content and graphics to demonstrate what the completed course might look like.

# What Do You Think?

**Which prototype format do you prefer to use and why?**

_____

_____

_____

**When does it make sense to use a wireframe prototype?**

A wireframe prototype is ideal when you need to focus solely on the technical functionality of your eLearning course. For example, if you're wanting to develop a complex interaction or branching scenario, it can be helpful to quickly build it in your eLearning authoring tool, using placeholder images, graphics, and even content.

*An example wireframe prototype, demonstrating the functionality of a custom interaction, with placeholder content and images.*

## When does it make sense to use a visual prototype?

A visual prototype is ideal when you need to focus on the look and feel of your eLearning course. For example, if you're working with specific design and branding guidelines, it can be helpful to design your slides with the required text, images, graphics, and layouts to see how they look. This is true, even if you're working with placeholder content.

*An example visual prototype, demonstrating overall look and feel of the course visual design, with placeholder content.*

**When does it make sense to use a functional prototype?**

A functional prototype is ideal when you need to showcase a sampling of the total learning experience, including the content, the interactivity, and the visual design. For example, if you need to give your stakeholders and subject matter experts a preview of the course for their approval, it can be helpful to create a fully developed functional prototype.

*An example functional prototype, demonstrating the overall course experience, with real content and images.*

# Review, Revise, & Repeat

Once you've developed your prototype, you'll need to get feedback from your stakeholders and subject matter experts. As we explored in the previous chapter, reviewing and iterating your eLearning course is an important part of the development process. What you don't want to do is lock yourself away for several weeks, developing the whole course, without giving your reviewers a chance to check in on your progress.

**Help your stakeholders understand how to review your course.**

When you deliver each draft of your course to your stakeholders, remember to explain what they're receiving and what you need from their review. During the prototype and development stage, you're no longer looking for feedback on the content but rather the presentation of the content, the interactivity, and the overall visual design.

**Make sure you have the right people reviewing your course.**

As you plan out each of your review cycles, make sure you're including the right people at the right time. Ideally, you'll have already determined this when you created your project plan and timeline; however, your stakeholders are likely to invite additional folks into the review process. Don't let this take you by surprise. Be proactive and find out who these people are and include them in the process.

**Continue iterating until you've developed the whole course.**

After you've completed the initial review of your prototype, continue iterating on the development of the course, incorporating any edits you receive from your stakeholders. From this point, you're now headed into the full development of the course. Continue building out the slides from your storyboard and reviewing with your stakeholders.

## How many review cycles should I include during the development of my course?

While there are no strict rules for when or how often you should send your course off for review, in my experience, a minimum of three review cycles is usually sufficient. However, it's important to remember that every project is different. Depending on the complexity of the course and the number of reviewers, you may need additional review cycles.

**1**   **First Review Cycle**   The first review cycle is for your stakeholders and SMEs to provide feedback on the course prototype.

**2**   **Second Review Cycle**   The second review cycle is for your stakeholders and SMEs to provide feedback on the first draft of the fully-developed course, with incorporated feedback from the first review cycle.

**3**   **Third Review Cycle**   The third review cycle is for your stakeholders and SMEs to provide sign-off on the final draft of the course, with incorporated feedback from the second review cycle.

# What Do You Think?

**How many review cycles do you typically include in your development process?**

_____

_____

_____

NOTES

# INCORPORATE INTERACTIVITY

---

**In this chapter, you'll explore...**

- The benefits of interactive eLearning.

- The different types of interactivity.

- How to create performance-based interactions.

---

## NOTES

---
---
---
---
---
---
---
---
---
---
---
---
---
---
---
---
---
---
---
---

# INCORPORATE INTERACTIVITY

**Let your learners put their skills into practice.**

Interactivity plays an important role in creating engaging and effective eLearning. Unlike synchronous learning experiences (i.e., instructor-led training), asynchronous eLearning depends on interactivity to keep the learner engaged and to help put concepts into practice.

Whether your learner is clicking a button to advance to the next slide, clicking a tab to reveal additional content, or selecting a response to a scenario-based question, interactivity is any action your learner takes within your eLearning course.

However, I must admit, the importance of creating interactive eLearning wasn't something I learned quickly. When I first started as an eLearning designer, I remember being constantly reminded of the importance of making my eLearning content interactive. I was told that interactive eLearning equaled engaging eLearning. To be 100% honest, when I look back on my early work as an eLearning designer, I can say that I had no idea what I was doing!

As a new eLearning designer, I figured the purpose of interactivity was to help maintain and engage the learner's attention—as long as the learner was required to click on something, it would keep them "engaged" in the course. And so, that's exactly how I designed my eLearning courses.

Several of my very first eLearning courses included content that was organized into simple, click-to-reveal interactions. Whether it was a series of tabbed buttons or pulsing icons, all of the interactions were essentially the same: the learner would click a button, and it would reveal some content for the learner to digest.

## Knowledge and behavior aren't mutually exclusive.

The truth is, it wasn't until I was required to sit through an eLearning course that was full of click-to-reveal interactions that I started thinking about whether my eLearning interactions were meaningful or passive. I quickly realized that I was designing eLearning interactions that were simply displaying additional information for the learner to consume—rather than helping drive performance by having the learner apply the skills being taught.

This is because knowledge and behavior aren't mutually exclusive. You can make a highly-interactive course, but if all that's happening is the learner clicking to reveal additional information, then you can't expect the learner to actually develop any skills that will be applied back on the job!

## What Are the Benefits of Interactivity?

While it's not required for all eLearning to be interactive (or effective), depending on your desired learning and performance outcomes, interactivity can help your learners put their skills into practice. Just like you might include activities in a classroom workshop, the goal isn't to simply transfer knowledge but rather to enable your learners with the skills, behaviors, and tasks they'll need to perform on the job.

**Here are just some of the benefits interactive eLearning has to offer...**

- **Interactivity can promote critical thinking.**
  Interactive eLearning can challenge your learners to face real-world problems, situations, and scenarios. This lets your learners practice their skills in a safe environment.

- **Interactivity can provide a sense of accomplishment.**
  Interactive eLearning can let your learners see the outcomes of their decisions. When they make the right decisions, this can boost their confidence and provide a sense of accomplishment.

- **Interactivity can encourage reflection.**
  Interactive eLearning can let your learners experience the outcomes of making the wrong decisions, without facing the real-world consequences. In turn, this can encourage your learners to reflect on their skills and abilities.

# What Do You Think?

**Do you incorporate interactivity into your eLearning? What are some other benefits of interactivity?**

_____

_____

_____

## Considerations for Creating Interactivity

Although we know interactivity can help learners put their skills into practice, this doesn't mean every eLearning course requires interactivity.

For example, if you're creating a short how-to video, explaining how to log in to a system, there may be no need for interactivity. This type of situation may not warrant a hands-on practice within the training environment because the practice will take place later, when the learner actually attempts to log in to the system.

On the other hand, if you're creating a course, teaching sales employees how to overcome customer objections, it might make sense to create a series of scenario-based questions.

Regardless of the situation, it's important to consider the complexity of the course you're building and whether or not it aligns with the content and the learning outcomes you're seeking to achieve.

## The complexity of your eLearning course should be fit for function.

The eLearning course you build should be fit for function. This means only investing the time necessary to achieve the desired results. Otherwise, you risk wasting your (and your learners') time, building something that is excessively complex.

In other words, it doesn't make sense to build a complex interaction for a simple task and vice versa. As you seek to incorporate interactivity, there are several considerations you need to take into account, each affecting the overall development of your eLearning course.

**When designing interactivity, ask yourself the following...**

What are the desired learning & performance outcomes?

The complexity of interactivity you incorporate into your eLearning course should align with the learning and performance outcomes you're seeking to achieve.

What other opportunities will the learner have for practice?

If you're designing a blended training solution, make sure to consider what other opportunities for practice your learner will have during the training experience or on the job.

How much time do I have to develop the interactivity?

Consider how much time you have to develop your course and the interactivity. If you're short on time, consider how you can adjust the complexity of the interactivity to meet your needs, without comprising the learning experience.

Is my eLearning authoring tool capable of creating the interactivity?

Not all eLearning authoring tools allow for complex or custom forms of interactivity. Make sure to consider what you can and cannot accomplish with the tool you're using.

# What Do You Think?

**What other considerations might affect the types of interactivity you include in your eLearning course?**

_____

_____

_____

# Types of Interactivity

Before you can decide how to make your course interactive, you need to understand how the different types of interactivity compare to one another.

With all of the benefits interactivity can offer your learner when they take your eLearning course, it's important to note that not all interactivity is the same. While most interactivity will require the learner to take some sort of action within your eLearning course, different types of interactivity will have different types of learning outcomes. In other words, not all interactivity is created equally.

**In our industry, interactivity is usually categorized into four levels of complexity...**

### 1

### Passive

Limited or no user interaction beyond slide controls (i.e., Next button).

### 2

### Limited

Simple, click-to-reveal interactions.

### 3

### Moderate

Decision-based scenarios and simulations, requiring use of critical thinking skills.

### 4

### Complex

Advanced, fully immersive simulations (i.e., AR & VR).

### What's the difference between click-to-reveal and decision-based interactions?

While the complexity of your interactivity can range from passive to complex, most interactivity included in asynchronous eLearning falls into two categories: click-to-reveal interactions and decision-based interactions. While each type of interaction has its place within the creation of an eLearning course, it's important to understand how each one does or does not promote learning.

As I explained at the beginning of this chapter, you can make a highly interactive course, but if all you're using are click-to-reveal interactions, then you can't expect your learners to actually develop any skills that will be applied back on the job.

---

### When it comes to asynchronous eLearning, most interactions fall into two categories...

#### Click-to-Reveal Interactions

Click-to-reveal interactions are any type of interaction where the learner clicks a button or takes an action to reveal additional content or resources, whether it be text, audio, video, or something else.

While click-to-reveal interactions won't challenge your learner's critical thinking skills, that doesn't mean they can't add value to your eLearning course.

#### Decision-Based Interactions

Decision-based interactions are any type of interaction where the learner must use their critical thinking skills to make a decision within your eLearning course.

Whether it's a simple multiple-choice quiz or a complex branching scenario, decision-based interactions challenge your learners to put the skills you've taught them into practice.

**When does it make sense to use click-to-reveal interactions?**

Click-to-reveal interactions are ideal when you need to simply transfer knowledge to your learners by organizing information into multiple steps or processes. They're also beneficial when paired with decision-based interactions, providing additional resources or information when they might need it the most.

While I believe that click-to-reveal interactions have their place, it's important to remember that they simply don't allow the learner to apply their critical thinking skills. In other words, the only knowledge or skills the learner needs to apply to complete a click-to-reveal interaction is the use of their mouse and nothing more.

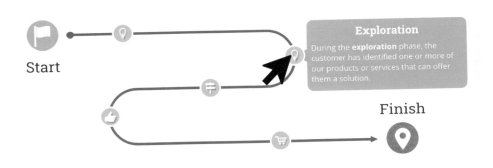

*An example of a labeled graphic interaction, letting the learner explore multiple steps in a process.*

# Our Customers

We provide products and services to many different customers, with many different needs. Click each customer to learn more.

## The Experienced Executive

—

Experienced executives are pragmatic and discerning. They are looking for long-term solutions, along with long-term results. While they may be impressed by brand credibility, it must be accompanied by solid data.

*An example of a pop-up window interaction, letting the learner reveal additional information about each on-screen character.*

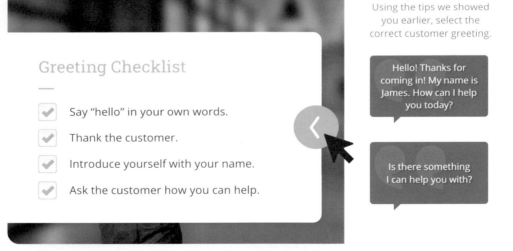

*An example of a slide-out interaction, letting the learner reveal additional resources to assist in the completion of a decision-based interaction.*

When designing eLearning interactions, it's easy to become overwhelmed trying to envision the actions the learner will take, how you'll build them in your eLearning authoring tool, and if they'll actually be effective.

Over the years, I've learned the best methods for designing eLearning interactions are to think visually and remove any sense of technical limitations. This usually results in creative solutions that wouldn't have occurred to me otherwise. Here are three simple tips for brainstorming and designing eLearning interactions...

### Sketch Your Ideas

When you're storyboarding your eLearning content, it's not always easy to describe a complex interaction on paper. And even if you do manage to write it all out, it can be helpful to visualize your ideas first. When designing your eLearning interactions, try sketching your ideas. If possible, find a whiteboard and get away from your desk and computer.

### Focus on Behaviors

eLearning interactions come in all shapes and sizes—some are as simple as the learner clicking to reveal content, and others are complex learning scenarios with multiple branches. When designing your eLearning interactions, focus on the real-life behaviors you want the learner to emulate back on the job.

### Ignore Technical Limitations

One of the biggest barriers to designing eLearning interactions is thinking through and overcoming technical limitations. When designing your eLearning interactions, ignore your technical limitations—don't worry how or if you'll be able to build these interactions in your eLearning authoring tool. The goal of brainstorming your eLearning interactions is to think outside of the box. Once you've finished generating your ideas, you can worry about the technical aspects when building an eLearning prototype.

**When does it make sense to use decision-based interactions?**

Decision-based interactions are ideal when you want to challenge your learner to use their critical thinking skills to make some sort of choice or take some action. Whether it's a simple multiple-choice question or a complex branching scenario, decision-based interactions should be designed to help your learners achieve a specific performance objective.

Ideally, decision-based interactions are based on real-life situations or scenarios, that present your learner with real-life choices and outcomes.

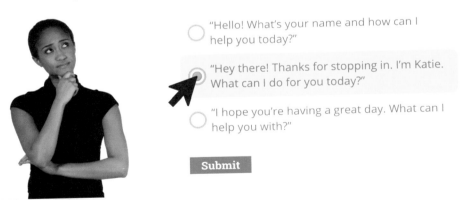

## Let's Check Your Knowledge

Select the correct response. Which of the following statement includes all of the required elements for greeting our customers?

○ "Hello! What's your name and how can I help you today?"

◉ "Hey there! Thanks for stopping in. I'm Katie. What can I do for you today?"

○ "I hope you're having a great day. What can I help you with?"

**Submit**

*An example of a basic, multiple-choice question, challenging the learner to select the correct response.*

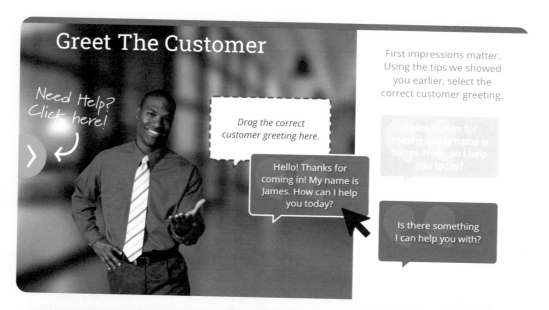

*An example of a drag-and-drop scenario interaction, challenging the learner to select the correct response.*

# How Would You Respond?

A customer calls to ask about a mysterious charge on their monthly bill. Using the customer service skills we showed you earlier, respond to the customer and see what happens.

Thanks for calling today! How can I help?

Customer

There's an extra charge on my bill for last month.

You

**Response 01**

I'll need to transfer you to the billing department.

**Response 02**

Sorry for the confusion. I'm happy to help. Let's take a look.

**Response 03**

Got it. I'm going to put you on hold for a few minutes.

**Response 04**

Are you sure it's not a normal charge on your monthly bill?

---

# How Would You Respond?

A customer calls to ask about a mysterious charge on their monthly bill. Using the customer service skills we showed you earlier, respond to the customer and see what happens.

**Great Job!**

Yes! The best response is to simply let the customer know that you're there to help them.

That would be great. Thanks for your help!

**Response 01**

I'll need to transfer you to the billing department.

**That's Right!**

You selected the correct response.

**Continue**

**Response 03**

Got it. I'm going to put you on hold for a few minutes.

**Response 04**

Are you sure it's not a normal charge on your monthly bill?

*An example of a branching scenario question, challenging the learner to select the correct response.*

When compared to click-to-reveal interactions, designing decision-based interactions can be much more time consuming. Here are two practical tips you can use for designing meaningful, decision-based interactions, focused on performance...

## Focus Your Content on Performance

My first tip for designing decision-based eLearning interactions has nothing to do with interactivity, but rather the nature of your course content. You see, one of the biggest hurdles to designing meaningful interactivity starts with whether or not you're trying to solve a gap in knowledge or a gap in performance. Trust me, there's a big difference!

The first step to designing decision-based eLearning interactions is to make sure your course is focused on performance and behaviors. What is it that your learners need to do to achieve the desired performance outcome? Once you have an understanding of the specific behaviors you're looking to affect with your eLearning course, you can then target your eLearning interactions towards those behaviors.

## Design Interactions to Put Behaviors Into Practice

My second tip for designing decision-based eLearning interactions is to allow the learner to put the desired behaviors into practice. This is the key element that differentiates a knowledge-based eLearning course from a performance-based eLearning course.

For example, let's say I needed to create an eLearning course on how to respond to an angry customer. One example would be to create an interactive scenario where the learner needs to deescalate an angry customer by selecting the appropriate response, using the skills they had been taught previously. Depending on how the learner responds to the angry customer, the scenario could branch to a series of different outcomes. Through this, the learner could apply the skills being taught in an experiential way, without fear of failure. And if they do fail, they can see (and learn from) the consequences of their actions, without fear of retribution.

# What Do You Think?

**What kinds of click-to-reveal interactions do you include in your eLearning content?**

_____

_____

_____

**What kinds of decision-based interactions do you include in your eLearning content?**

_____

_____

_____

**What other types of interactivity do you include in your eLearning content?**

_____

_____

_____

**If you could redesign any of your past courses, how would you design the interactivity differently?**

_____

_____

_____

# NOTES

# INCREASE LEARNING RETENTION

---

**In this chapter, you'll explore...**

- Sweller's Cognitive Load Theory.

- How to reduce cognitive load.

- How to design engaging and intuitive eLearning.

---

NOTES

# INCREASE LEARNING RETENTION

**Good eLearning is more than just good instructional design.**

In the previous chapter, we explored how you can build interactivity into your eLearning content. When designed properly, interactivity can have a huge impact on how your learners retain the knowledge and skills taught during your course. However, interactivity alone isn't the only way to increase learning retention.

Asynchronous eLearning is a form of interactive multimedia, which lets you combine text with images, graphics, animations, and audio to convey your training content. And when you take the time to consider how these elements can be combined to elevate your message and content, it gives you the power to create a visually engaging and immersive experience.

While there are a number of ways to improve the effectiveness of your eLearning content, in this chapter, we'll look at what I consider the top ways you can reduce cognitive load and increase learning retention when designing your course.

## Do You Remember How Learning Occurs?

Earlier in this book, we talked about how learning occurs. As human beings, we're constantly taking in and processing information. Whether you're reading a book, watching a video, or practicing a skill, we are always learning. It's part of the human condition—to coin a phrase.

However, let me ask you this: do you recall everything you did last week? How about everything you read in the last eight chapters of this book? The answer is most certainly no!

## Although we're always learning, it doesn't mean we're always remembering.

Our brains are programmed to automatically process and prioritize information. Some information is retained only for the amount of time necessary to complete a task, and then it's forgotten. In other situations, information is kept for the long term.

Let me give you an example. Throughout my entire education as a child and into early adulthood, I absolutely hated math, especially algebra! For me, I was perfectly content using a calculator for the rest of my life, as long as it meant I didn't have to learn algebra.

During my second year in college, I was required to take my very last algebra class. While I hated the experience, I did everything I could to pass. I studied my butt off, memorized the order of operations for every equation, and I managed to pass the final with a C+. I was relieved to say the least! However, if you had asked me to take the same final exam a few weeks later, I guarantee I would have failed.

Why is this? Well, it's because it simply wasn't important to me. Subconsciously, my mind only needed to retain the information necessary to pass that test. Once that was accomplished, that information no longer served a purpose and was forgotten.

What does this have to do with learning? Well, when you create training, the minds of your learners are subconsciously prioritizing that information. Depending on how much content is being received, how it's being presented, and whether or not it's relevant to your learners, that information is either retained for long-term memory or dumped once the training event is over. This is where John Sweller's cognitive load theory comes into play.

# John Sweller

In the late 1980s, John Sweller developed cognitive load theory while studying learners and how they solved problems. As a result of his research, Sweller concluded that learning is most effective when it occurs under conditions that are aligned with the human cognitive architecture.

Sweller's theory suggests that short- and long-term memories are organized into "schemas," or a combination of elements, which form the whole of an individual's knowledge base. This means information that is retained in long-term memory is structured as complex schemas, which allow us to perceive, think, and solve problems.

From an instructional design perspective, information is initially processed by working memory, before it is retained into long-term memory as a schema. Sweller's cognitive load theory suggests that we should design our training content to reduce the amount of load placed on the working memory, allowing the mind to generate schemas and retain information for the long term.

**John Sweller**

*An Australian educational physiologist, best known for formulating the theory of cognitive load.*

## As a result of his research, Sweller identified three types of cognitive load...

### Intrinsic

Intrinsic cognitive load is created by the inherent level of difficulty associated with a specific instructional topic.

### Extraneous

Extraneous cognitive load is created by the manner in which information is presented to learners and is under the control of instructional designers.

### Germane

Germane cognitive load is created by the processing, construction, and automation of schemas.

## How Can Cognitive Overload Be Reduced?

If I asked you what makes an eLearning course effective, how would you answer? Would you say instructional design? I'm sure you would—that's what most folks say! However, good eLearning is more than just good instructional design. As I explained earlier, eLearning is a form of interactive multimedia, which lets you combine text with images, graphics, animations, and audio to convey your training content.

## Good eLearning is more than just good instructional design.

While it's impossible to completely avoid cognitive overload, there are ways it can be reduced. As we explored on the previous page, out of the three types of cognitive load, extraneous cognitive load is the one we, as instructional designers, can avoid by how we present information to our learners.

And while there are countless ways I could explain how to effectively present information to your learners, for the remainder of this chapter, I want to explore what I think are the top four methods you should consider...

- How you structure your content.
- How you make your content visually engaging.
- How you show the concepts you're trying to explain.
- How you design your course to be intuitive.

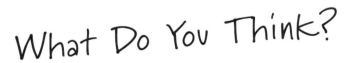

**What are some other ways you can avoid cognitive overload?**

_____

_____

_____

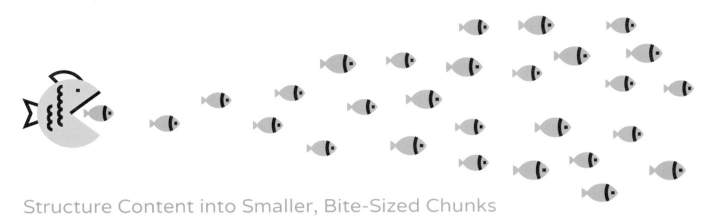

## Structure Content into Smaller, Bite-Sized Chunks

Over the years, our industry has attempted to define guidelines for the ideal length of an eLearning course. Some folks say an eLearning course shouldn't exceed 45 minutes, others say 20 minutes, and nowadays, I hear people say 10 minutes. And as I explained earlier, I've never been a firm believer that an eLearning course should be restricted to an arbitrary duration of time. I've always believed that an eLearning course should be as short or as long as it needs to be to cover the required content.

An eLearning course should be as short or as long as it needs to be to cover the required learning content.

However, this isn't to say that you shouldn't be strategic or thoughtful about how you chunk or scaffold your training content. Even if you have a 45-minute eLearning course, it doesn't mean you should try to cram 25 new concepts into that one course. Depending on the nature of what's being taught, you want to avoid overloading the learner with too much information or too many concepts at once.

To avoid this, you can reduce cognitive load in eLearning by structuring the learning content into smaller, bite-sized chunks. For example, if you have five new concepts or behaviors you need to teach your learners, and they each will take about 10 minutes to cover, you could build a single 50-minute course; however, it's not likely that your learners will retain all of the information. On the other hand, you could chunk each concept into five, shorter eLearning courses, with each being 10 minutes in duration.

## Design Slides to Be Visually Engaging

Here's some truth for you: humans are visual creatures! We eat with our eyes first, we fall in love with our eyes first, and we learn with our eyes first. It's because of this that graphic design in eLearning matters! When I first started in eLearning, I put all my efforts into instructional design. Although I wanted my courses to look better, I really only worried about graphic design if I had the extra time at the end of a project.

Humans are visual creatures! We eat with our eyes first, we fall in love with our eyes first, and we learn with our eyes first.

You can reduce cognitive load in eLearning by using basic graphic design techniques. Learn what colors and fonts work well together, select high-quality and relevant images and graphics, and create a clean and balanced layout. Practicing good graphic design techniques doesn't mean learning how to create custom graphics. Sometimes it's just a matter of moving things around on the screen until they look good.

Cheesy
stock
photo

Default
fonts

What is our customer
service philosophy?

We seek to empower our
customers with products,
services and solutions
that solves their problems
—some of which they
may not even realize.

VS

### What is Our Customer Service Philosophy?

—

We seek to empower our customers
with products, services and solutions
that solves their problems—some of
which they may not even realize.

Realistic
imagery

Contrasting
typogrphy &
colors

Simple
layout

## Show the Concepts You're Trying to Explain

When I first started developing eLearning courses, I remember thinking that my slides were merely there for me to insert the content of my course. Although many of my first eLearning courses included audio narration, all it did was simply repeat all of the content I included on the slides, word-for-word.

## Use your slides to help your learners see what you're trying to say.

I've since realized that eLearning is a tool for visual communication—it's an opportunity for you to create a multimedia experience for your learners—one that incorporates graphics, audio, animations, interactivity, etc.

You can reduce cognitive load in eLearning by pairing meaningful graphics with animations and audio narration. Rather than throwing a bunch of bullet points and generic stock photos on your slides, use your slides to visualize the concepts you're attempting to explain. For example, if you're teaching a new process, visualize the process with a diagram or series of icons, animating each step as it's explained by the audio narration.

# The Customer Journey

During the sales process, you can get a sense of your customer's motivations, needs and pain points. To do this, we follow a five-step customer service process.

1. **Discovery:** During the discovery phase, the customer is still exploring their options. They are not committed to our company, brand, services or products.
2. **Exploration:** During the exploration phase, the customer has identified one or more of our products or services that can offer them a solution.
3. **Comparison:** During the comparison phase, the customer explores how our product or services compares to the competition.
4. **Evaluation:** During the evaluation phase, the customer has decided our product or service is the right one.
5. **Purchase:** During the purchase phase, the customer has finally decided to commit to our brand, product or service.

*Boring bullet points*

*No imagery*

 VS

# The Customer Journey

During the sales process, you can get a sense of your customer's motivations, needs and pain points. To do this, we follow a five-step customer service process.

*Simple text*

Discovery

Exploration

**Comparison**

Evaluation

Purchase

*Meaningful graphics*

## Design an Intuitive User Interface

When I first started creating eLearning courses, I didn't need to worry about designing an intuitive user interface. At the time, I was using Articulate Studio, which simply converted my PowerPoint slides into Flash-based eLearning courses. By adding a player with a menu and navigation controls, the user interface was taken care of for me. However, nowadays, with tools like Articulate Storyline and others, the ability to create custom, on-screen navigation is easier than ever.

When designing an interactive eLearning course, it's crucial that you make the experience as intuitive as possible. For every second your learner spends trying to learn how to use your course, it's a second they aren't learning the concepts you're trying to teach.

## If you have to explain how to use your course, it's not that easy to use!

You can reduce cognitive load in your eLearning by designing an intuitive and easy-to-navigate user interface. Keep the navigation of your course simple and consistent. Make sure your buttons look and behave like buttons. Where possible, reduce the number of clicks to complete a specific task. And of course, conduct user acceptance testing (which we'll explore later) to get feedback on the usability of your eLearning course.

*Excessive & confusing navigation* ↘

MENU GLOSSARY NOTES

Consultative Sales 1010

▸ Our Customers

▸ Consultation Basics

▸ Building Rapport

▸ Offering a Solution

▸ Closing the Sale

RESOURCES

## Main Menu

Learn more about our customer service philosophy and process by selecting a topic below.

- 👥 **OUR CUSTOMERS**
- ⚙️ **CONSULTATION BASICS**
- 💬 BUILDING RAPPORT
- ⚜️ OFFERING A SOLUTION
- 🤝 CLOSING THE SALE

⏮ ▶ ──────────────── ↻ ‹ PREV    NEXT ›

**VS**

## Main Menu

Learn more about our customer service philosophy and process by selecting a topic below.

- 👥 **OUR CUSTOMERS**
- ⚙️ **CONSULTATION BASICS**
- 💬 BUILDING RAPPORT
- ⚜️ OFFERING A SOLUTION
- 🤝 CLOSING THE SALE

*Simple navigation* ↗

# LAUNCH & MEASURE YOUR COURSE

---

**In this chapter, you'll explore...**

- How to conduct a quality assurance check.

- How to deliver your eLearning course.

- Kirckpatrick's Four Levels of Evaluation.

---

NOTES

CHAPTER TEN

# LAUNCH & MEASURE YOUR COURSE

**It's time to set your course free...almost!**

Well, you've been waiting for this moment for a long time! After weeks, and maybe even months of hard work, endless review cycles, and iterations of development, you're now ready to publish your course and make it available to your learners.

How you ultimately deliver your eLearning course to your learners largely depends on your organization. It's likely you'll be publishing your course into a Learning Management System (LMS) for tracking purposes.

However, at this point in the design and development process, there's still a lot to be done! Before you publish your course, you need to conduct a quality assurance test (and possibly a user acceptance test) to make sure your course is 100% ready-to-go. After you publish your course, you need to measure its effectiveness and wrap up your project by conducting a retrospective.

# Conduct a Quality Assurance Check

Up until this point, you've been working your butt off designing and developing your course and reviewing it with stakeholders and subject matter experts. You've spent time refining the learning content, building scenarios, and visually communicating your ideas. Now, you're nearly ready to launch your eLearning course to your learners.

But is your course really ready for prime time? Well, you don't want to risk launching your course to hundreds, or even thousands, of learners to discover you missed a typo, or worse, something that doesn't work properly! The best way to avoid this embarrassment is to thoroughly conduct a quality assurance check.

## You should QA your eLearning course early and often.

Quality assurance, or QA testing, is the process of reviewing your eLearning course to identify any outstanding errors, typos, or other glitches that must be fixed before the course is published. Although I am a big advocate of QA testing early and often, you should always QA your course once you are done with development and before you deliver it to your learners.

---

**Quality assurance testing can help you identify...**

| | |
|---|---|
| *Spelling & Grammar Errors* | While many spelling and grammar errors should have been resolved during the storyboard stage, you still want to double-check and fix any lingering typos. |
| *Technical Functionality Glitches* | If you've created a complex eLearning course, you want to make sure it works as intended. This means checking all of your buttons, links, or any other interactive content. |
| *Visual Design Inconsistencies* | Check the visual design of your course to ensure you've been consistent with fonts, that objects are properly aligned and distributed, and that everything looks polished. |

---

## What other strategies can I use to QA my course?

- **Take a break from looking at your course.**
  The more often you work on your course, the less likely you are to spot errors. During your QA testing process, take a break from looking at your course and give yourself as much time as possible between development and QA.

- **Get a second set of eyes.**
  Sometimes the best people to help you review your eLearning course are those who have never seen it in the first place! During your QA testing process, get a second (and possibly a third) set of eyes to look at your course. Pick someone who hasn't been involved with the development of your eLearning course and let them review it.

- **Try to break your course.**
  Most errors in an eLearning course are discovered when learners try to do what they aren't supposed to do. During your QA testing process, put yourself in the shoes of your learners and do the unexpected—try to "break" your course. For example, if you're QA-ing a slide where you are supposed to select a single item, see what happens if you select multiple items.

# What Do You Think?

**What else do you need to QA before launching your course?**

_____

_____

_____

## Facilitate User Acceptance Testing

In the last section, we explored how you can identify errors within your eLearning course by conducting a quality assurance check. While a good QA check will help you identify the majority of your errors, sometimes it's your end users (the learners) who spot the mistakes.

Additionally, wouldn't it be nice to see how your learners might react to your eLearning course before you launch it? Well, you can do this by facilitating a user acceptance testing (UAT) session with a select group of your learners.

**User acceptance testing can help you identify...**

| | |
|---|---|
| Usability Issues | Are several of your testers getting stuck in the same spot of your course? If so, something might be broken or confusing. |
| Content Concerns | Do several of your testers disagree with the content? If so, something might be inaccurate or irrelevant. |
| Learner Reaction | How are your testers reacting to the course? Debrief with your testers to find out what they liked and disliked. |

# What Do You Think?

**What are some other benefits of conducting user acceptance testing?**

_____

_____

_____

## What are some tips for facilitating user acceptance testing?

- **Gather a diverse mix of testers.**
  Start by gathering a diverse mix of testers. Ideally, you want to create a test group that matches the diversity within your target audience.

- **Don't explain how to use the course.**
  Do not explain how to use the course they're testing. Let your testers interact with the course on their own. By doing this, you'll quickly identify what areas of the course might need additional work.

- **Observe and take notes.**
  Observe and take note of how your testers are struggling; that way, you can later refine those areas of the course before publishing.

- **Debrief and ask questions.**
  Once your learners have successfully (or unsuccessfully) completed the course, debrief and ask questions. If any of your testers got stuck, find out why. If they were able to get unstuck, find out how. This is also an excellent time to see how your testers responded to the learning content.

- **Don't justify your design decisions.**
  No matter what your testers say, resist the urge to justify your design decisions. The goal is to learn from your testers to improve the design of your course, not to correct what they did or did not do wrong during the testing process.

- **Prioritize and implement the feedback you receive.**
  The goal of user acceptance testing is to get feedback that you can use to improve your course. After you've completed your testing, sort through the feedback and prioritize what's most important to fix. If your testers discovered usability issues, make sure to fix those first. If your testers didn't respond well to the content or didn't find it helpful, determine what specific changes you can make to improve it.

# Decide How You Want to Deliver Your Course

One of the most important decisions when wrapping up your eLearning project is deciding how you want to deliver it to your learners. Most eLearning authoring tools offer several options for publishing your course, and which one you use will depend on your organization, whether or not you need to track completion of the course, and what technology is available.

**There are two primary methods for delivering your eLearning course...**

LMS

Publishing your course for delivery via a Learning Management System (LMS), lets you assign the course to your learners and track completion rates. Typically, publishing to an LMS means publishing your course to the SCORM, AICC, or Tin Can API standards.

Web

Publishing your course for delivery via the web lets you deliver your course to nearly anyone with internet access. Unlike publishing for an LMS, when you publish for the web, you typically lose the ability to track who has completed your course. Publishing for web delivery typically means publishing your course to the HTLM5 standard.

# What Do You Think?

**How will you be delivering your eLearning courses to your learners?**

_____

_____

_____

## What is SCORM, AICC, xAPI, & HTML5?

It can feel a bit overwhelming when you hear things like SCORM or HTML5; however, all you need to know is that they reference the back-end technology used to deliver your course.

- **SCORM, AICC, and xAPI (sometimes called Tin Can API)** are technical standards used by most eLearning authoring tools and learning management systems. Publishing your course to the right standards will ensure your course "plays nice" with your LMS.

- **HTML5** is a coding language used by most modern websites. Before HTML5, most eLearning courses were published to the Flash standard. However, as of December 2020, Adobe is retiring Flash and most web browsers will no longer support Flash-based content.

## What if I'm still not sure how to deliver my course?

If you're still not sure how to publish and deliver your course to your learners, you should meet with your LMS administrator, who should be able to help you properly publish and prepare your course for delivery. If you don't have an LMS admin but still need to get into your LMS, I would then suggest reaching out to your LMS vendor, who can provide specific instructions for publishing eLearning content into your LMS.

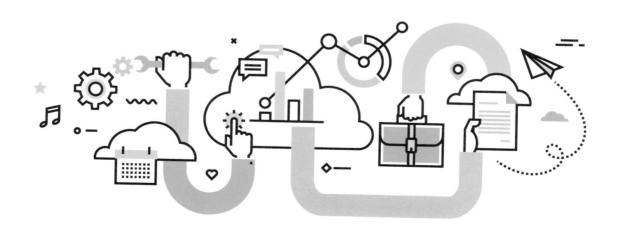

# Measure the Effectiveness & Impact of Your Course

After you launch your course to your learners, whether it's just a single eLearning course or a blended training solution, it's important to measure the effectiveness and impact of your work.

- Did your learners enjoy the training?

- Did the training teach your learners anything new?

- Did the training help your learners change their behaviors?

- Did the training achieve the results you sought to achieve?

These are all questions you want to be able to answer after you delivered your training solution. Otherwise, you run the risk of never knowing whether or not your work is doing any good. This is where Kirkpatrick's Four Levels of Evaluation can come in handy!

**Donald Kirkpatrick**

*A United States professor, best known for creating the "four level" model for training evaluation.*

## Donald Kirkpatrick

In late 1954, Dr. Donald Kirkpatrick wrote his Ph.D. dissertation on evaluating training for industrial supervisors. As a result, Kirkpatrick's work was distributed to a larger audience in 1959, when he wrote a series of articles for the US Training and Development Journal. Then in 1994, Kirkpatrick's work became widely recognized within the industry, upon the publication of his book entitled *Evaluating Training Programs*.

Kirkpatrick's four levels are designed as a sequential method of evaluating training programs, starting with learner reaction and ending with business results.

Typically, as one progresses from one level of evaluation to the next, the evaluation process becomes more difficult and requires more time.

**As a result of his work, Kirkpatrick defined the four levels of evaluation...**

### Reaction

The degree to which participants find the training favorable, engaging and relevant to their jobs.

### Learning

The degree to which participants acquire the intended knowledge, skills, attitude, confidence, and commitment based on their participation in the training.

### Behavior

The degree to which participants apply what they learned during training when they are back on the job.

### Results

The degree to which targeted outcomes occur as a result of the training and support.

# What Do You Think?

**How do you currently measure the effectiveness of your training content?**

_____

_____

_____

## Measure Learner Reaction

Level one evaluations seek to measure the degree to which participants find the training favorable, engaging, and relevant to their jobs. Typically, learner reaction is the easiest evaluation to complete. The most common method for measuring learner reaction is by soliciting feedback via a post-course survey.

While learner reaction data won't say much about whether or not the course was actually effective (a course doesn't have to be enjoyable to be effective), you can still glean important information that can help you improve the overall learning experience.

As you review your learner reaction data, look for anything that can help you identify whether or not the training was a good use of your learners' time. Did they use the information presented in the course? Would they recommend the course to their colleagues?

# What Do You Think?

**Do you measure learner reaction? If so, how do you collect the data, and what do you do with it?**

_____

_____

_____

## Measure Learner Knowledge

Level two evaluations seek to measure the degree to which participants acquire the intended knowledge, skills, attitude, confidence, and commitment based on their participation in the training. Typically, learner knowledge is measured by providing a pre- and post-test to determine what new information was gained.

While learner knowledge data can help you identify what information your learners remembered after completing the course, it still lacks the ability to tell you whether or not your learners adopted the skills taught in the course. This is because, as we explored earlier, knowledge and behavior aren't mutually exclusive.

As you review your learner knowledge data, look for anything that can help you design better content. For example, if several learners consistently get a specific question wrong, you may want to investigate how you can improve the instructional design of that content.

# What Do You Think?

**Do you measure learner knowledge? If so, how do you collect the data, and what do you do with it?**

_____

_____

_____

## Measure Learner Behavior

Level three evaluations seek to measure the degree to which participants apply what they learned during training when they are back on the job. Typically, learner behavior is measured either through specific performance metrics or by direct observation.

Depending on what skills (if any) you taught during your course, it can be more difficult to measure learner behavior. Whether you measure via performance metrics or by direct observation, look for any specific changes that can be correlated back to the completion of your course.

One way to accomplish this is by conducting an A/B test, with only half of your learners completing the course. This can help you identify whether or not your course actually resulted in a change in behavior.

## What Do You Think?

**Do you measure learner behavior? If so, how do you collect the data, and what do you do with it?**

_____

_____

_____

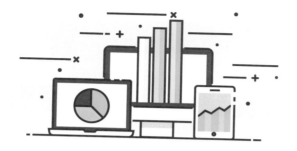

## Measure Business Results

Level four evaluations seek to measure the degree to which targeted outcomes occur as a result of the training and support. Typically, business results are measured by correlating the specific skills taught in your course to specific business outcomes. This is done by analyzing any specific performance metrics available.

Ideally, your course has some direct relation to the business results you're seeking to achieve. This is where writing good learning and performance objectives can help. The more specific they are, the easier they are to measure.

Similar to measuring learner behavior, the biggest challenge is validating whether or not your course is the reason why performance improved. Again, this can be done with an A/B test.

## What Do You Think?

**Do you measure business results? If so, how do you collect the data, and what do you do with it?**

_____

_____

_____

# Conduct a Project Retrospective

When you finish a project, and before you move onto the next one, it's a good idea to reflect on the successes (and failures) of your last project. By skipping this process, you're missing a tremendous opportunity to learn from the past and improve in the future. This is where a project retrospective can help.

Whether you call it a retrospective, postmortem, debriefing, or wrap-up, the purpose of an eLearning project retrospective is simple: to help you and your team evaluate your performance and processes and hopefully improve them in the future.

**Conduct a project retrospective by answering these three simple questions...**

*What did we accomplish?*

Start your retrospective by reviewing the project and course. Take a few moments to cover the goals, budget, timeline, audience, constraints, etc. The goal is to give a thorough history of the project, from start to finish. If you have time, take a moment to look through the course to showcase the final deliverable(s).

*What did & did not go well?*

After you review the project, the next step is to discuss what did and didn't go well. Remember, the purpose of the retrospective is to learn from and improve your development process. This is your opportunity to have an open conversation about the project, those involved, and the end result.

*What will we do differently next time?*

The final step is to identify specific actions you will take to improve your development process in the future. Sometimes, it's not always clear what the right answer is to fix the issues you might identify. The goal is to experiment with small tweaks and modifications to your process and then evaluate them at your next retrospective.

Who should I include in my project retrospective?

You can conduct your project retrospective with as many or as few people as you'd like; however, it's my preference to include anyone who contributed to the project. This might include your stakeholders, subject matter experts, or anyone else who participated in the kickoff meeting.

# What Do You Think?

**Do you typically conduct a retrospective at the end of your projects?
If so, who do you invite and what do you discuss?**

_____

_____

_____

_____

# KEEP GOING!

**Becoming a good eLearning designer requires a lot of practice.**

While we've covered a lot of ground about the eLearning development process in this book, there's still a ton left for you to learn! I'd like to use this closing chapter to share some lessons I've learned over the years that have helped me become a better eLearning designer—with the hope that they help you as much as they've helped me.

To start, let me say this: not everyone is cut out to be an eLearning designer. I don't say this to discourage you, but rather, to be honest about the amount of effort required to become a good eLearning designer. During my first year in eLearning, I really struggled. I didn't fully realize and respect the skills and practice required to be a good eLearning designer.

## Get Outside Your Comfort Zone

It wasn't until I pushed myself outside my comfort zone that I started to grow. I forced myself to research the fundamentals of good instructional design, the use of good graphic design techniques, and everything in between. These efforts eventually paid off.

Good eLearning designers aren't good because they're cut out for it, but rather, because they put in the practice needed to become good at it!

Your comfort zone.

Where the magic happens!

## Design eLearning Even When You're Not Getting Paid

Let me start by saying that I don't mean you should work for free! Becoming a successful eLearning designer requires you to practice your craft. Although you'll get a lot of practice working on eLearning projects at work, it's not always enough to expand your skills and talent.

Successful eLearning designers invest their extra time designing eLearning on their own. It might seem crazy, but doing this provides an opportunity to create content you otherwise might not with projects at work. This enables you to flex and build your creative muscles. It also offers you the opportunity to build your portfolio. The truth is, if you aren't willing to design eLearning on your own time to improve your skills, you might want to rethink how passionate you really are about becoming an eLearning designer!

## Share Everything You Know

I've been working in the eLearning industry for more than a decade. In that time, my success as an eLearning designer hasn't been due to the number of eLearning courses I've created or the number of books I've read. My success as an eLearning designer is largely due to the community of designers within the eLearning industry.

I've benefited directly from others who have been so gracious to share everything they know. Over the years, I've tried my best to do the same: to share everything I know with people like you and the rest of the community.

By helping and inspiring others with my knowledge, I've also helped myself. Sharing everything I know has helped me create a blog, speak at conferences, and even write this book. It's helped me snag amazing jobs, new clients, and new friends.

*Here I am with Ashley Chiasson in 2016, attending the DevLearn Conference & Expo in Las Vegas, Nevada.*

## Be an Expert Of Your Experience

Despite the benefits of sharing everything you know, it's not always an easy thing to do. In fact, it's downright scary! When I first started in eLearning, I didn't think I had the authority to share my knowledge with others. Who was I to have an eLearning blog or speak at an eLearning conference?!

That changed for me when I mustered the courage to speak at my very first eLearning conference in March of 2014. I spoke at the Learning Solutions Conference & Expo on the ten things I learned during my first year in eLearning.

I thought the presentation went horribly; however, I was shocked by the number of people who approached me after my session to thank me for sharing my story.

It was then that I realized that I didn't need to be an expert in eLearning to be an "expert" in eLearning—I just needed to be an expert of my own experiences!

## Fake It Until You ~~Make~~ Become It

I started this book by telling you that I'm not really an eLearning designer—just someone who happens to play one at work. The truth is, I've been faking it the entire time! Because I didn't grow up dreaming of becoming an eLearning designer or go to college to earn a prestigious degree in instructional design, I've had to fake my way through it all.

Unless you went to school to become an eLearning designer (which most of you didn't), you've had or will have to fake it, too—and that's okay! I'm living proof that you can fake it until you become it.

## Let Me Know What You Think

I hope you enjoyed reading *The eLearning Designer's Handbook*! For me, this book was a personal journey, an item checked off my bucket list, and a huge accomplishment. Self-publishing a book takes a lot of time and effort. Not only was I the author of *The eLearning Designer's Handbook*, but I was also the editor, formatter, designer, marketer, and much more. The success of this book depends on the reviews and ratings it receives on Amazon.

If you liked *The eLearning Designer's Handbook*, please take a few minutes to write a short review and rate the book on Amazon. Every review helps! :)

## Acknowledgments

I owe thanks to more people than I could possibly list here. I owe thanks to the folks who not only helped lift and push me through each stage of my career, but also those who made sacrifices that enabled this book to become a reality.

Brandon, thank you for giving me the time and space to write this book, sacrificing many of our evenings and weekends.

Jessica and Sue, thank you for taking a chance on me early in my career. It was your decision to choose me that radically changed the trajectory of my career.

Diane, thank you for teaching me everything I needed to know to self-publish a book.

## Thanks for Reading

Well, that's it, folks! I want to thank you for reading the second edition of *The eLearning Designer's Handbook*! I hope you enjoyed reading it as much as I enjoyed writing it! This book has been several years in the making, and I'm so happy it's finally done and available for you to enjoy!

As you reflect on what you've learned, I want to encourage you to do what I've attempted to do in this book: share your experiences with others. There's always someone who is in need of your help or guidance, and you never know when a new eLearning designer might be looking to you as an expert!

Made in the USA
Columbia, SC
02 January 2024